D1368447

WHERE LOVE AND FRIENDSHIP DWELT

LOUISE SWANTON BELLOC
from a drawing by Hilaire Belloc in 1932

WHERE LOVE
and
FRIENDSHIP DWELT

~~~~~~

BY

Mrs. Belloc Lowndes

AUTHOR OF

"I, TOO, HAVE LIVED IN ARCADIA"

"Un livre est une épitre écrite à des amis inconnus"

~~~~~~

NEW YORK : 1943

Dodd, Mead & Company

Copyright, 1943
By MARIE BELLOC LOWNDES

ALL RIGHTS RESERVED
NO PART OF THIS BOOK MAY BE REPRODUCED IN ANY FORM
WITHOUT PERMISSION IN WRITING FROM THE PUBLISHER

PRINTED IN THE UNITED STATES OF AMERICA
BY THE VAIL-BALLOU PRESS, INC., BINGHAMTON, N. Y.

928.2
L91

97-4966
877061

FOREWORD

WHERE Love and Friendship Dwelt tells of my
return, at the age of seventeen, to my French
home, and describes certain people and certain
of my relations who played a considerable part
in my early life. I also deal, in this book, with
friendships made by me in the Paris of the late
eighties and early nineties of the last century.

M. B. L.

LIST OF ILLUSTRATIONS

WHERE LOVE AND FRIENDSHIP DWELT

I

AFTER the death of my English grandmother, Mrs. Parkes, in 1877, our life in London came to an end, for we moved to Slindon, a beautiful village in Sussex. There I never felt happy, for life in the English countryside of those days was too different from anything I had known to provide anything in the way of interest and amusement to the thoughtful, thinking child I had become. I was more content during the two years I spent at Mayfield, where the nuns belonging to the Order of the Holy Child then had a school for girls under fourteen. I have retained a most affectionate and grateful feeling for many of the nuns, some of whom were remarkable and cultivated women; but while at school, I felt keenly the separation from my mother.

My French grandmother, Madame Swanton Belloc, died when I was thirteen, and during the four years which followed, we lived almost entirely at Slindon. The fact that my mother's income had become very small meant I could take but little part in the way of life of the young people with whom I was thrown. They were all kind to me, and I became fond of them; but each autumn and winter cub-hunting and hunting filled their days, while I was then, what I have remained during the whole of my life, only concerned with, and interested in, literature, and various forms of art.

Meanwhile my brother, Hilaire, had been sent to school at the Oratory. My mother chose the Oratory because of her great regard for Cardinal Newman. Hilaire generally acted in a Latin play which was given each year, and we were always asked to be present. These, and other visits to the Oratory, were agreeable breaks in my otherwise dull existence.

Now and again, but more and more rarely, we would go to Paris for a few days, almost always to be present at a family funeral or a family wedding; but that only made me look back the more longingly at the happy life I had led in my French home, constantly in touch with relations I loved, and who loved me.

And then, in the spring of 1885, my mother suddenly decided we should spend the summer at La Celle Saint Cloud. She had a chance of letting her house at Slindon, and I think she had come to understand, in a dim way, how much I wished to be once more in France, and in touch with my own people.

I know, now, how she must have shrunk from again taking up life in the place where she had known the only deep happiness she had experienced. She had married at the age of thirty-seven, and my father had died just five years later. I also realize, now, how painfully anxious she must have been that my two aunts, and the large circle composed of old friends and acquaintances of the Belloc family, should remain unaware of her changed financial circumstances. Owing to her trust in a friend's son, who was part owner of a firm of outside brokers, she had lost the whole of the considerable sum of money which had been left to her by her father's brother, shortly before she became a widow.

Much as I loved her, we were too different the one from the other for me to understand my mother's extremely peculiar nature and character. I cannot remember her ever speaking to me in any intimate sense, during my early youth, of her five ideal years of married life with my father. Nor can I remember a single allusion as to how much she missed the constant care, and thoughtful unselfish love, which had been lavished on her without stint by her husband's mother, during the nine years following his death. Yet, though she seldom cried, I remember seeing her burst into bitter tears when she found by chance a note, written in English, addressed to me by Madame Swanton Belloc, when I was eight years old. It ran:

"My dear little Marie, I do not wish your Mamma to tire herself by writing to me. But it seems some time since I had news of her, and the last time it was only on a postcard. Will you write me a few lines, dear child? You need only say in it, 'Mamma is well', or 'Mamma has not been well, but is better now'. I wish to know the exact truth about her dear health, and I am sure Nurse will help you with the letter, and tell you what to write, without troubling your mother. You see, my dear, I have to trust to your kind little heart in order to be well and regularly informed. And now, God bless you, my darling; also your beloved mother, and Hilaire."

Though I had been selfishly overwhelmed with an almost painful sense of joy the day we left Slindon for some months, it was in a sense both sad and strange coming back to an empty silent house which had always been filled, during my childhood, with the friends of my French grandmother. In those days it had echoed with eager talk and laughter, for my first cousins were high-spirited and, at that time of their lives, free from care. Though all of them were considerably older than I and my brother, they were still very young before the first phase of our French life had come to an end.

Madame Swanton Belloc and my mother had had three excellent maids and a young manservant. Now, with the exception of a woman who came in to cook our lunch, wash up, and prepare a very simple evening meal, the elderly woman who had been our nurse, and I myself, did everything.

My mother had at once arranged to sleep in what was called

the annexe, which consisted of three bedrooms and a dressing-room, over our *grand salon*. It was there Hilaire and I, with one of the maids, before Nurse had come to us, had slept as little children. My parents had only inhabited the annexe for a few weeks after their marriage before moving into the châlet, a tiny house built some thirty years before, on part of what had been my grandparents' garden.

And now Nurse was also in the annexe and, as for me, I selected the charming room Mademoiselle de Montgolfier, my grandmother's friend of fifty years, had occupied every summer, since the year the Hilaire Bellocs had bought the property.

This room, which commanded a delightful view of the château, and of the park and gardens where I had spent many hours of almost every day as a child, was exactly as it had been left, that is in perfect order, after being occupied during the autumn and winter of 1870–71 by successive German officers. The interior of the rest of the house, and everything that had been in it, had been practically destroyed, or else stolen and sent to Germany.

We found the village itself quite unchanged, and every house had, if not the same inhabitant, then some member of a family I had known all my life. But to my mother's distress, what had been a high hill covered with chestnut groves, affording a beautiful prospect from all our windows, now had, close to the summit, a railway station. It was on the direct route to Marly-le-Roi, and round it were grouped a number of ugly new buildings. Yet, thanks to this station, we were within an hour of Paris; but no road leading to it had been built; and it could only be reached from our house after half an hour's hard walking, first down a very steep stony cart-road, and then up a steeper, narrower track. So all the La Cellois who had carriages, still drove to Saint Cloud in preference to using the new station. To us it was to prove a real boon, and a considerable economy. There were but

two classes on the suburban lines; the difference in price was small, and all our friends went first class as a matter of course. It was characteristic of my mother that we always traveled second, often in company with live cocks, hens, ducks, and big hampers of fruit and vegetables, on their way to certain of the Paris shops or markets.

I had naturally walked everywhere alone at Slindon, and when we arrived at La Celle Saint Cloud, I assumed I should do the same. My mother, fortunately for me, did not realize the surprise and disapproval which would be aroused by my doing such a thing, for all the girls I was so soon to meet were always accompanied everywhere either by a relation or by a maid, even if the distance to be walked was only a few yards.

On our first morning, I left my mother writing letters, and I started, without telling her where I was going, on two short pilgrimages. The first was to our *cimetière*. The last time I had walked up the rough path leading to the wide gate, I had formed part of a considerable concourse of people who had been present at Madame Swanton Belloc's funeral. At that time, though already very anxious and distressed concerning my mother's money troubles, I had been a child; now I was on the eve of my seventeenth birthday, and felt myself to be quite grown up.

Just opposite the gate of the *cimetière* of La Celle Saint Cloud are our family graves. At that time, at the head of the centre grave stood a marble cross left, by my mother's wish, with neither name nor date, where my father lay buried. Adelaide de Montgolfier, his godmother, who had loved him as if he had been her son, is in the same grave; his mother lies to his right.

I knelt down, said prayers for all their souls, and then I gazed at the graves of men and women I had known as a child, before finally making my way to the corner where were buried three unknown Prussian soldiers who had died during the first German occupation of the village. To these graves our mother had

always brought me and my brother, to lay flowers on All Souls' Day.

I then went along to the woodland path, close to our house, where stood a humble monument where three peasants had been shot, in 1871, for cutting telegraph lines. Knowing what the Germans have done in the last two years, I think it probable the monument is no longer there. So I should like to put on record the last words uttered by the oldest of these men, just before he was shot. They were engraved beneath the three names, and ran: *"Je suis Français. Je dois tout entreprendre contre vous. Si vous me rendez à la liberté, je recommencerai."*

During that summer, La Celle Saint Cloud seemed, to me, like Paradise; all the more so, though I was not aware of it, because in a sense everything, excepting the enchanting background, was changed. Young people lived in many of the houses where I had only known old people. Girls of much my own age were now at the château; and at Les Bruyères, where a childless diplomat, the Comte de Circourt, a family friend I did not much like, had been succeeded by a brother with two granddaughters. The villa Béranger had been let to a Paris banker, with a pleasant wife, and several sons and daughters. Thus I became at once part of a highly vitalized group of young people who met daily at each other's houses, while every Sunday afternoon a small informal dance took place at the château, to which were invited certain of the St. Cyr cadets, comrades of the fiancé of one of the girls who lived at Les Bruyères.

How odd, indeed how dull, would my young English neighbours in Sussex have regarded those Sunday dances, yet how I enjoyed them!

Each of us took it in turn to work a kind of primitive hurdy-gurdy which stood in the corner of the large, square, glass-paned room, which must once have been a winter garden. It was reached

from the drawing-room of the château, and a glazed door led to a terrace which, had the house been an English country house, would have been covered between each dance, with girls and their partners. But I do not remember any of us ever going out there, for, though never mentioned, the French rules as to chaperonage were strictly observed. As I remember, there were never more than eight to ten couples, and we depended entirely for young men on St. Cyr. The military academy is a long way from La Celle Saint Cloud, and our partners used to ride over, tethering their horses in the riding-school which is one of the features of the château. At the end of the afternoon, a delicious *collation* was served in the dining-room; but there were only soft drinks.

The whole of my former life at La Celle had centred, to a considerable degree, round the château and its owners. Madame Dutreux was very tall, very slight, and very active. As early as five on a summer morning I would go across to my window, and see her walking in her vast, indeed magnificent, kitchen garden which was filled with flowers, as well as with every kind of fruit and vegetable. It lay between our house and the high trees which partly masked the château.

Madame Dutreux's three grandchildren, two girls and a boy, were as dear to me as if they had been my sisters and my brother. As for their mother, I loved her dearly; she was one of the most delightful human beings I have ever known. Long after her death I wrote to her younger daughter:

"I wonder if you realize the part 'Madame Emma' played in my existence when I was a child and girl. There radiated from her such an exceptional atmosphere of kindness and goodness, and she possessed such a high distinction of mind and thought. In my now long life I have never met anyone recalling her peculiar personality. Then, again, how extraordinarily vivid are my recollections of your grandmother! I was always a little afraid of her, while being exceedingly fond of her. The other night I dreamed of her; I heard her intensely individual voice welcoming me as she had so often done at the front entrance of the château, and then she walked away with a gliding motion, her elegant figure as if floating through the great rooms towards your grandfather's tiny kidney-shaped study, which was then entered by a concealed door in the drawing-room."

Monsieur Dutreux subscribed to a great many weekly publications, and was always ready to lend me any of his papers and magazines. The one I preferred was *L'Intermédière*, the French opposite number to *Notes and Queries*, for I have always enjoyed reading out-of-the-way and curious pieces of information.

The château of La Celle Saint Cloud had been owned by Madame de Pompadour, though only for a comparatively short time; yet she had had a miniature copy of the fountains at Versailles made in the park at an immense cost. But of these *grandes eaux* nothing remained after the Revolution. Again, not only in her day, but for long afterwards, the château could only be approached from Versailles through the woods, by a road which is now grassed over, though it is still lined by rows of magnificent trees which were among the few spared by the Germans during the winter of 1870–71.

My mother suddenly discovered with dismay I had quite forgotten how to read French; so she forbade me to read any English books for two months. But—and this was an example of how her mind worked—I could read any French book I liked, excepting *La Nouvelle Héloïse* and *Les Trois Mousquetaires*. I have never read either of these famous books to this day. She had remembered that *La Nouvelle Héloïse* was supposed in the France of my father's day to fill the hearts of not only girls, but of young men too, with an ideal of love impossible of attain-

ment in this strange world. As for *Les Trois Mousquetaires*, she had always felt disgust for the character of Miladi. But had I come across Balzac's *Contes drolatiques* and Casanova's memoirs, they could have formed part of my holiday reading. I did actually read, during that summer, and in the succeeding years, all Balzac's novels, all those of Dumas *père* (excepting *Les Trois Mousquetaires*), and every contemporary French novel I could beg or borrow. But I was well aware of how restricted is the reading of French girls, and I kept the fact that I could read anything I chose, to myself.

I also began to try and write some aricles at that time, and I earned thirty shillings for a paper describing little known aspects of Versailles. Both my reading, and my attempts at writing, were approved by my mother, but she had no understanding of, and no sympathy with, my pleasure in young society.

Looking back, I fear all her waking moments that summer were filled with pain, and an anguished longing for the past. There is even now a solitary road, called locally *la route de Versailles,* bounded on one side by splendid woods, and on the other by the eighteenth-century wall of the château, which has always vividly recalled certain walks during which my poor Mamma, as I and my brother always called her, would impress on me of how she disliked, and even despised, the changed France to which she had come back. She must have written to my Aunt Lily, Madame Ballot, telling her of how unhappy she felt at finding everything so different from what it had been, and how fearfully she missed her husband's mother; for in answer came a long letter, of which I give the conclusion:

"God compels us to face up to unexpected happenings, and to vast changes in our lives which, at the time they occur, appear unnecessary. But there is nothing to do, my dear dear sister, but to submit; and this is specially true if, like you and me, a woman has children. I miss our mother as much to-day as I did just after her death. But I know it would not have been a good thing, even if it could have occurred, for her life to have been prolonged.

"For young people to live in the shadow of old age is bad—believe me it is. From what you tell me, the French girls with whom Marie is now thrown in contact for the first time are not undesirable companions, though that you find them uninteresting is natural. I have no special liking, I might go further and say I have no understanding, of most of my Marcel's friends. But I welcome them to my house, and I am careful never to criticize them to him in any way—though I hear plenty of criticism of them from Marcel's father! What matters to me is that my son should love and trust me, and I feel sure that in your heart you have the same sentiment with regard to Hilaire and Marie."

There was, however, one place in the village where Mamma felt at ease, and was even, at times, happy. This was the house of the only first cousin who still, in the dark days of war while I am writing this simple chronicle, is alive, and living in what was till last autumn Unoccupied France.

Of Juliette Siry, the only daughter of my Aunt Louise, and of my uncle, Jacques Redelsperger, were once written the words, "She appears as restful and as serene as is a perfect spring day." At the time I am attempting to describe this charming creature, her husband, a clever and cultivated man of whom I became extremely fond, and their five little children, lived in a villa, called *La Vallée des Lys*. The villa stood on a plateau at the top of a wooded hill, well outside the village, though within a quarter of an hour's walk from our house. Étienne Siry had wide business interests, and was a wealthy man. He was interested in everything that was going on in the world excepting, alas, as like in that to all Frenchmen of his generation, and of the generation which followed, the French political world.

Though they often had friends out from Paris, and made expeditions in what was an exceptionally romantic and historically interesting neighbourhood, the life as led by the Sirys in their country house, might well have seemed dull to a young English or American couple of their kind. Tennis, which was just beginning to be played in France, was the only outdoor game. They had, however, one pleasure hardly known in the England of so many lovely streams and rivers. Juliette, her husband, any one staying in the house, and the now joyous Marie Belloc, used to drive *en bande,* as the saying went, to bathe and swim from an island in the Seine, a little way from Bougival, at a place absurdly called *Le Petit Trouville.* There, had been built a group of primitive bathing huts, and a stretch of the river was corded off. Beyond the water so curbed, no one was supposed to swim, for there was a good deal of traffic on the Seine, even large boats going from Paris to the sea.

My mother and I had a standing invitation to dinner at the Vallée des Lys. What I most enjoyed in these dear people's house was the lively eager talk, especially when, by some happy chance, either of my first cousins, Jacques Redelsperger, Juliette's brother, or Marcel Ballot, Aunt Lily's son, came out from Paris. Though entirely different the one from the other, each of them had inherited the effortless wit of our grandfather, Hilaire Belloc. They also heard all the news there was to hear, for each of them formed part of the literary, theatrical, and diplomatic worlds then known as *Tout Paris.* On quieter evenings, Étienne Siry would read aloud a play, or be coaxed into an eager discussion by his English aunt (who spoke excellent French) concerning some political event which she wondered aroused so little, if indeed, any, comment, from the French people with whom she came in contact. And then there were Juliette's two boys and three girls; a constant source of interest and amusement to me, for till then I had never known any small children.

Who, then, would have thought it conceivable that the eldest of those five fortunate little creatures would take part in a terrible war, and be killed, after having been twice so severely wounded that his parents each time were told he could not possibly live. His brother died shortly after 1918, as a result of the hard fighting he had done, and the privations he had endured. As to the three little girls, who led on a more luxurious scale much the same delightful life I had led as a child, they were all happily married by 1914, and all of them went through four years of wretched suspense. The husband of the second daughter was posted as missing in the October of 1914, and his wife thought she had reason for hoping he might be a prisoner, until at last his grave was found. None of the three men were soldiers. One was a banker, and the other two were successful members of what are called the liberal professions.

I would like to add that Étienne Siry happened to be mayor of La Celle Saint Cloud during 1915, and all that frightful winter he kept many of the old men, women, and children of the village alive, by rushing lorries of food from Paris—for there was sheer starvation in districts which were apparently at once too near, and too far, from the capital, for relief to be properly organized. Having carried out that useful task, which he kept up long after his year of office, this fine-natured Frenchman died, soon after the end of the war, worn out with hard work, and with grief at the loss of his two sons, and of a son-in-law of whom he had been proud and fond.

But in the eighties of the last century France felt profoundly at peace. *La Guerre* (of 1870–71)—still the only war to the average Frenchman—seemed to be forgotten, at any rate among the educated classes. My cousin Juliette's children were taught German, as well as English, and their father had business relations with Germany. The owner of the finest property in the neighbourhood had married a German lady, and everyone who had the good fortune to know her, loved her. Even the older people in the village close to the château where she dwelt part of each year—those to whom *l'Année terrible* had brought such miseries and humiliation—preferred Madame Tony, as she was called, to her husband's mother. I remember feeling thankful Madame Tony had died before the summer of 1914.

My Aunt Lily spent with us my seventeenth birthday, and the same evening she wrote to my mother:

"It made me so happy to be to-day at La Celle Saint Cloud, in that old house of such mingled associations. You and I have had eighteen years of close affection, of complete confidence, and of common memories. We always understand one another without any word being spoken, and we have the same hopes for your son and for your daughter. And you, I know, dear sister, take the tenderest interest in my two sons. I often feel anxious about their future, for it seems to me that our old French world is crumbling about our feet, or perhaps I ought to say that every day I fear some kind of earthquake. Indeed sometimes I feel I hear ominous sounds issuing from our body politic.

"Last night I remembered, with such a curious sense of reality, my own and my brother's childhood and youth. Involuntarily I compared the France in which we then dwelt with that of to-day. You know the quiet old-fashioned set of people in which I live with my husband,—and yet how often do I hear such words as 'What exactly is his position?' 'How much money have they?' 'It is said he has made a million on the Bourse,' etc. etc. My brother Louis and I never heard any phrase of that kind uttered in our presence. Inasmuch as there was ever talk concerning our friends, though there was not much talk of the kind, for my parents were not particularly interested in people, we would be told of their intelligence and of their talents. Such virtues as loyalty, delicacy, and kindness were brought to our notice. If we heard of the vices of a man or a woman, they were real vices, not mean little sins. And the question as to whether a person was rich or poor did not arise, and so was never mentioned. Oh, Bessie, I often feel such a strong nostalgia for that vanished world."

II

ALTHOUGH we seldom spoke of her, both to my mother and myself, the airy, sunny rooms of my French home still seemed filled with the presence of my grandmother. She had been the living centre of the house for more than half my life, and when I went into the *grand salon,* I longed to see her tall figure come slowly through one of the doors, or from the white rose wreathed wooden balcony.

My room was opposite to that in which I used to go and see her each morning in my childhood and it had been left exactly the same as when she had occupied it. Like most Frenchwomen of her generation she lived much in her bedroom, and there she did all her writing. Feeling as I now did—that is completely changed from a happy, unquestioning child to a thoughtful questioning young woman—for I was years older in mind than my actual age, I constantly thought of my dear *Grand'mère,* and wondered what she had been really like. I was the more concerned with her personality because I was supposed—in my view quite untruly—to be extremely like her, both in appearance and in character. And, as time has gone on, especially during the last three years, I have become more, rather than less, interested in what remains in my mind as an enigmatic human being.

Louise Swanton Belloc died sixty-one years ago, yet I remember her as if I had seen her yesterday. But I feel I know very little about her, in spite of the hundreds of letters I have read written by her to my mother during the fourteen winters which preceded her death; indeed I know less about her than I do concerning the nature and character of many historical characters.

My French grandmother was completely lacking in the effusiveness characteristic of many Frenchwomen. I do not remember her, for instance, ever kissing me, excepting when bidding me good-morning or good-night. Neither can I recall hearing her bestow on my mother any of the endearing epithets which abounded in all the letters she wrote to one she loved with so deep and moving a love. In daily life she was not only extremely dignified in appearance; her manner was aloof; and her fine face was set in grave lines.

To please her English daughter-in-law, she put down, not long before her death, a fragmentary account of her early life from the time when her parents settled in Paris after her father, the last colonel of the Berwick Brigade, had left the army, till she and my grandfather, Hilaire Belloc, made what was to be their lifelong Paris home in the heart of the *Quartier Latin,* on the left bank of the Seine.

The third, and now the only unmarried daughter of a stern, and very old-fashioned, soldier, of whom she had always been the favourite child, she was then nineteen and allusions to her exceptional loveliness are to be found in several French memoirs. Madame de Quirilles, an English lady married to a Frenchman, wrote long afterwards, "As a girl Louise Swanton was an entrancing vision of beauty; and, as time went on, she resembled a Madonna, keeping her perfect features, and placid serene expression."

The Marquise de la Villette, Voltaire's *"Belle et Bonne,"* had let a small pavilion in her garden to Colonel and Madame Swanton, and Louise soon became a dear younger friend of the old lady, and was always invited to her celebrated receptions. But the girl enjoyed far more the hours she spent alone with *Belle et Bonne,* for it was then she would hear curious, often strange, stories, about Voltaire. One such, which I have never seen in any account of him, was that on Saint Bartholomew's Day he always stayed in bed as a sign of mourning, refusing to receive even the most intimate of his friends. The marquise was surrounded by relics of Voltaire, and she always sat in the armchair in which he had sat when writing his *Henriade*. On a table within reach of her hand was a gold box which contained his embalmed heart; and his bust was so placed that whenever she looked up, she could see his sardonic face.

The Marquise de la Villette received her remarkable circle of acquaintances, and foreigners who came with introductions from all over the world, three times a week: and when she was herself an old woman, Madame Swanton Belloc once compared the reception room of *Belle et Bonne* to a magic lantern across whose illuminated surface there passed, and repassed, all the famous figures of the Paris of her youth.

Meanwhile, Madame Swanton became a friend of Miss Patterson, the American wife of Jerome Bonaparte, and she also met, and became attached to, Madame de Montholon, who had been at Saint Helena. The memory of Napoleon was revered by Colonel Swanton; and one of the things I vividly remember concerning my grandmother, is that she had retained a strong feeling not only of immense admiration, but of something like personal affection, for *l'Empereur*. She would never tolerate a word against him said in her presence, and the only time in thirteen years I remember seeing her angry—and her anger on this occasion was formidable—was when she found our English nurse reading a children's story which gave a most unflattering picture of that great man. She disliked what she knew of Napoleon the Third, and had a slight prejudice against the Empress Eugenie.

Colonel Swanton's womankind must have found him difficult to live with at this time of his life, for he had an extremely obstinate character, and was accustomed to instant obedience. He had early determined his youngest daughter should become the wife of one of her brother's fellow officers. Although she had no dowry, three of these gentlemen, after the Swantons had settled in Paris, ardently wished to marry her. But she had begun to write when she was seventeen and, to the indignant surprise of her father, she expressed her firm intention of remaining single.

Time went on; she had formed a friendship by letter with Maria Edgeworth, and was translating that writer's stories for young people, and so beginning to earn a little money when, at the age of twenty-two, she met at a friend's house a painter named Hilaire Belloc. Though he was ugly, she thought him, to use her own expression, distinguished in appearance, and she had experienced, when they were introduced, an odd feeling that this was not their first meeting. But he did not tell her, till a year later, how he had often waited, for what to him had seemed hours, to catch a few glimpses of her walking with her father across the Place Saint Sulpice.

To please him, his sister Madame Le Roy procured an introduction to Madame Swanton, and asked if her brother might paint her daughter's portrait. Madame Swanton would have been willing, but Colonel Swanton regarded such a request as highly impertinent. Even so, Hilaire and Louise saw each other, and had a short conversation, on three occasions, during the six months which followed.

Then came a formal visit from Monsieur Le Roy to inquire on behalf of his brother-in-law, if Louise Swanton would consent to become Hilaire Belloc's wife. Colonel Swanton was accustomed to receive such *demandes en mariage,* and he expected his daughter to make her usual answer. But this time, to her father's astonished displeasure, Louise expressed her willingness to marry a man who was only an artist, and thirteen years older than herself.

Their engagement lasted longer than is usual in France, owing to the fact that Louise's lover had no income, apart from that brought in by his painting. Still, there was more than a hope that a certain portion of what had been for over a hundred years the considerable fortune the Bellocs had acquired from vast sugar plantations in the French Indies, might come his way. The family, ruined first by the Napoleonic, and then by the British, blockade, had managed to retain a small interest in a large sugar refinery. But even this hope faded; and there came a day when Hilaire Belloc called on the old Colonel he knew hated the thought of accepting him as a son-in-law, to say that in view of what he had just learnt, he felt he should give Louise Swanton back her word. But, again to Colonel Swanton's anger, his daughter insisted on having a final meeting with Hilaire. Fifty years later she wrote:

"Our interview took place. I felt he loved me so truly, and he spoke in so noble a way, I could not but feel touched. So I told my parents that unfortunate as was the loss he had just sustained, that loss in no sense affected my intention to marry him."

Their wedding took place at Saint Sulpice, and the old soldiers of the Berwick Brigade filled the church.

During the first years of their marriage, the Hilaire Bellocs were so poor that after their eldest child, named after her mother, was born, they broke up their home in Paris. Louise and her baby went to Montmorency for the summer, while Hilaire took a studio in which he lived, only spending an occasional Sunday with his wife. But that autumn he was given three portrait commissions; and he must have possessed an optimistic nature, for at once they took a spacious *appartement* in a vast eighteenth century house, 5 rue de l'École de Médecine, which formed part of the Cour du Commerce. The street was extremely quiet, and their windows overlooked a large garden. Both their younger children, my father and my Aunt Lily, were born there, and during the forty years which followed, those rooms formed, in truth, an abode filled with love and friendship.

Owing to the destruction wrought by the Prussians in our house during the winter of 1870–71, practically nothing connected with the early life of Louise Swanton Belloc survives. But recently I found, with surprise and emotion, an envelope inscribed in my grandmother's handwriting "From me to my husband." There are but three letters, written when they had been married five years. Louise had been ill, and had been invited to spend her convalescence in a country house, near Orleans, belonging to some relations of her husband. The letters threw a new light on her character, and also showed me how very close was the tie which bound her to a man who must have been almost in every way not only very different from herself, but from any of the men she had met before her marriage.

In the France of those days, friends and acquaintances willingly acted as couriers, and each of the three letters was sent to Paris by hand. The young wife was evidently most anxious to save both paper and space, for the handwriting is smaller, far, than that with which I had become so familiar. Also, she used narrow sheets of that strong rag paper with which our forebears were blessed.

Though she was accompanied by the little girl who was to be their only child for eight years, she evidently felt exceedingly lonely apart from her husband. Each letter begins, *Mon cher bon ange* (a curious appellation I have never seen used elsewhere), and is filled with expressions of tenderness, and of her longing to be with him again. In one passage she describes a long delightful drive in the neighbourhood, and she adds it recalled the wedding journey "which held the happiest days of my life."

Even on her holiday, she was writing for long hours each day, working at a biography of Byron; correcting proofs of articles, and trying to think of new literary openings. Hilaire Belloc was painting portraits, while longing to paint pictures of a very different kind. His letters must have expressed anxiety, and a measure of discouragement, for in each of her replies she assures him that things will soon improve with them, and that nothing matters as long as they can both work, and be together.

The longest and most intimate of these three letters concludes with the words: *"Je te confie à Dieu, mon cher bon ange, Ta Louise."*

I do not think she cared, in a deep sense, for more than a very few men and women. But for those few she cared with all her heart and soul. It is difficult to find words which would not appear falsely exaggerated, to describe what she felt for my mother, her son's wife. A cold-natured, reserved diplomatist, who happened to have been in frequent touch with them both almost from the day of their first meeting, wrote, on hearing of her death:

"I felt a measure of surprise, as well as sincere grief, when I learnt that splendid soul is no longer with us. Her love and care for you formed the most touching relationship I have known during my long life."

Another letter, written at that same time, is, to me, of special interest, and came from Madame Souvestre. The Hilaire Bellocs both admired the novels, now long forgotten, of Émile Souvestre, and Madame Belloc was fond of the then very young Marie Souvestre, who is still affectionately remembered by many noted English and American women who were pupils at her famous school.

"Although we met so seldom of late years, your husband's mother meant so much to me, that I feel as if something has been torn out of my life. There was something in her character so noble and so selfless. I remember once going to see her at a time when she was fearfully anxious and unhappy, while my own life was full of happiness. On that day she put aside completely what was filling her heart, in order to rejoice with me."

To my aunt, Lily Ballot, came words of gratitude and grief from the then little known composer, Lalo. Twenty years before, he then being about forty, he had been reduced to earning his living by giving piano lessons. Among his pupils was the cherished only daughter of a wealthy cousin of Hilaire Belloc. The two fell deeply in love, to the indignant astonishment and horror of the girl's parents. They sought out my grandparents, and begged them to see Lalo, and make him realize his lack of delicacy. But the result of the interview was such that the Bellocs were touched by the romantic love the two had for one another, and warmly took their part. Hilaire Belloc told the girl's father she would miss the chance of real happiness if he and his wife persisted in refusing to allow her to marry Lalo. The marriage took place, and the Bellocs gave them as a wedding present a kit-kat portrait of my grandmother our family consider by far the most living portrait of her. The painted hand holds a letter on which are written a few words of affectionate congratulation to the couple she and her husband had befriended. Though Lalo was to remain unsuccessful till he was over sixty, he and his wife led an ideally happy married life. They are among the very few people for whom Léon Daudet, in his memoirs, had a good word, for he described them as "a delightful pair, united in an exquisite love." Lalo died five years after fame and fortune had come to him together. I never hear an air from his opera, *Le Roi d'Ys*, without that forgotten French romance coming into my mind.

During many weeks after Madame Belloc's death, Aunt Lily wrote to my mother every day, bringing a measure of consolation, and herself finding consolation in doing so. It was strange that her husband, Charles Ballot, who loved her with an absorbed and passionate love, was blind to Lily's sense of loss. Just before we went back to England after Madame Swanton Belloc's death, he said to my mother—for whom he had a kind of grudging affection, though they had nothing in common—that he was surprised to find how little affected his wife appeared to be. Yet the day before she had written:

"My dear dear sister, I don't know how I could go on living, with such a void in my heart, were it not that I am certain that the souls of those who loved us are allowed to be with us now and again. But many of those who mourn are like the disciples of our Lord at Emmaus; those we believe gone walk by our side, they even speak to us. But we do not know they are there, for we do not hear their voices.

"The Gospels have always meant much to me, and that special chapter, which once appeared obscure, now brings me comfort. The disciples not only loved Him, they must have often spoken of Him, and yet they were unaware that He came and walked by their side. There are times when I feel as if there hung a thick veil between my mother and myself, and then, suddenly, it is as though the veil were torn aside, and in a flash I feel she is here."

And a day or two later:

"I know it is illogical and selfish to have wished Maman's old age, with all the infirmities old age brings with it, to have been prolonged. Yet I miss her so sorely, that one of my reasons

-{ 23 }-

for wishing to live on has left me. Now and again I forget she is no longer nearby, and I say to myself, 'I must speak to Maman about that worrying affair, for she is the only human being whose advice will be worth asking.' And then comes the knowledge that I shall never again hear her voice—that voice which uttered strengthening words, filled with kindness and with love, at certain fearful moments of my life. Yet I ought not to repine, fortunate as I am in the never-ceasing affections and care not only of Charles, but of my darling son, Marcel. How could I go on if I were alone with myself? I only feel at peace during those hours when I can forget both the past and the present, in my painting. I am only happy when I am asleep. By the way I wonder if you ever heard what used to amuse me so, when I was a child? This was a story told of the Empress Marie Louise. She used to sleep and sleep and sleep; indeed people said that she could even sleep when she was standing up! I little thought I should ever come to envy her."

III

No account of my French grandmother should omit a few passages concerning Adelaide de Montgolfier. This lady was not only Louise Swanton Belloc's most intimate friend for close on sixty years, she collaborated with her in almost all her literary work; and she can be, I think, truly described as having been the most remarkable and gifted French spinster of the last century. Her versatility, to use a word now out of fashion, must have been extraordinary. She set verses of Béranger to music still sung in the village schools of France; and I possess a little book of pencilled portraits, drawn by her from life at meetings of the *Institut*, of noted Frenchmen and of famous foreigners, including Wellington, who were in Paris just after the Restoration. She spoke, read, and wrote, both English and German, and was evidently an amusing, as well as at times a brilliant, talker. She was small, slight, and graceful; and though her features were irregular, Victor Hugo described her face, after their first meeting, as filled with an *espiègle* charm.

Apart from her striking and unusual personality, the fact she was for many years the only surviving child of Étienne de Montgolfier, the inventor of the balloon, and a man who had been personally entertained and fêted by Louis the Sixteenth, caused many people in the Europe of her day to feel about her a certain curiosity, and she entertained, each winter, many Englishmen, Germans, and Russians. Among the Frenchmen who frequented her weekly receptions in the rooms where she spent each winter, were most of the writers of her long day, from Victor Hugo and

Sainte-Beuve, to Dumas *fils*, who was taken there by Émile Augier. Her letters, of which I have read many dozens addressed to my grandmother and to my father, prove how wide and diverse were her interests.

Louise Swanton Belloc made the acquaintance of Adelaide de Montgolfier and of Madame de Montgolfier soon after her marriage. Adelaide was nine years older than my grandmother, and, apart from their common interest in literature, few women belonging to the same country, and concerned with the same intellectual and literary interests, could have been more different. Yet they became, at once, dear friends, and from his birth, in 1830, Madmoiselle de Montgolfier had for my father what can only be described as an adoring affection. To his embarrassment, she woud sometimes recall with delight the fact that she was the first person who had ever held him in her arms, as she had been present when he was born. Her love for him was far more uncritical than that of his parents; indeed she regarded him as perfect. Never was this moving affection shown in a more striking way than when he married. Instead of being jealous of my mother, as would have been natural, and as every one round her expected her to be, she realized that he was at last completely happy. So she took his wife to her heart, and her joy at my birth, and that of my brother, was almost painful in its intensity. But my father's death, in August 1872, struck her body, soul, and spirit, mortal blows. From being a brilliant talker she became mute. From having been an eager reader of the literature of three countries, she no longer opened a book. Her sight, her hearing, and her power of movement were not affected, but in every other way she appeared to be another woman.

To go back, however, to the time when she was an outstanding personality in the literary and scientific world of Paris. Not only in the Belloc family was she always known as "Mademoiselle"; so she was always called by those who knew her in the world. My grandparents were both extremely busy and hard-working people, and had no time to spend in the company of men and women with whom they felt no special affinity. Mademoiselle, on her side, was always making new acquaintances, and enjoyed asking distinguished foreigners to lunch and dinner. But she appeared almost every morning in the study at 5 rue de l'École de Médecine, there to spend many hours sharing and discussing whatever literary work on which her friend happened to be then engaged. It was owing to her influence that Madame Swanton Belloc bent her fine mind to writing for the young, and together they edited the first children's magazine. This precursor of innumerable publications in Europe and America was called *La Ruche* (The Beehive). I think the fact that I was never even shown a number —though I later found several bound volumes in a cupboard— proves that my grandmother cannot have shared, in a serious sense, Mademoiselle's enthusiasm for what she called education. Though she always spent each summer as the guest of the Hilaire Bellocs at La Celle Saint Cloud, she kept in close touch with Annonay, the ancestral home of the de Montgolfiers, and she went there every year. Her heart and thoughts, however, were ever centred on Louise Swanton Belloc, and Louise's only son; and she certainly thought of herself as being the fairy godmother of the whole family.

As almost always happens in human life and with human beings, there was a very different side to the picture I have drawn of a devoted, and indeed nobly helpful, love and friendship. Of that other side I have become vividly aware as, through their letters, I have become closely acquainted with the group of people who formed the core of Adelaide de Montgolfier's life from the age of thirty-three, till her death exactly sixty years later.

All through their lives, her affection for Madame Swanton Belloc was threaded with strands of bitter jealousy; and she tried, more than once with success, to separate her from the other people who loved her. Her most serious, and also her one really successful, effort, was made after she had known my grandparents for a comparatively short time, and the person in question was Mary Clarke, who will live in the social history of France and England as Madame Mohl.

When the Swantons came to live in Paris, Mary Clarke had soon become their unmarried daughter's only young woman friend. They met daily, and to Louise Swanton the *salon* of Mrs. Clarke—dominated by her daughter Mary—brought sunlight and happiness into what was a shadowed life. Even then, Mary Clarke was already the centre of a circle composed of French writers, painters, and learned men, all famous in their way; and it is now known, through the publication of a number of letters which were kept by the man in question, that she had a secret, ardent love-affair with the philosopher-savant, Fauriel. Louise, who knew all Mary's secrets, was conversant with what was going on, and deeply sympathized with her friend's passionate desire to become Fauriel's wife. But he was very much older than the girl who loved him; he was set in his ways, and had no wish to change his condition. Intimate though they were, my grandmother only once alluded to this episode when speaking to my mother of her youth, and she did so in so veiled a way that my mother never guessed, and never knew, that the girl in question was known to her as Madame Mohl.

Mary Clarke seems to have had, when young, a dislike for women, the only exception being Louise Swanton. But after her marriage to Julius Mohl, the German scholar, she became the cherished friend of many distinguished Englishwomen, to whom she wrote admiring and most affectionate letters. With some of these ladies she frequently stayed in England, and she often entertained them in Paris.

To my mind a great deal has been written concerning Madame Mohl which is not only untrue, but absurd. In more than one account of her published since her death she was described as an almost angelic being, who only lived to do acts of kindness. Good-natured she certainly was, and at times what the French call *serviable;* as she grew older, however, she showed herself ruthless in eliminating people she had formerly known, and now thought of little account; also, as time went on, she only cultivated the socially important among those who came across her way. But while she was still young her generous instincts had not become atrophied, and she played an important part in the marriage of my French grandparents.

Shortly after Louise Swanton had become engaged to Hilaire Belloc, some spiteful person told her he was carrying on an intrigue with a wealthy widow who had long wished to marry him, and who hoped his engagement would come to an end. Astonished and disturbed, Louise took the opportunity, when alone with his married sister, to ask if there was any truth in the story. The answer seemed to her ambiguous and, as she was proud and sensitive, she at once decided to give up all thought of the marriage. In her great distress, for, even if she were not then aware of it, she had evidently come to care deeply for Hilaire Belloc, she said nothing to her parents, and only confided what had happened to Mary Clarke. Mary at once declared she felt quite sure the tale was untrue. And she did more. At a time when even in England such an action would have been regarded as extremely bold and unseemly, she went off, alone, to Hilaire's studio, and revealed what the girl he believed himself to be on the point of marrying had been told. He was deeply chagrined to learn Louise Swanton could have thought such a thing of him, and he told Mary Clarke the following circumstances. His sister had come across a rich young widow who wished to marry again, and she had introduced the two to one another. Not only had Hilaire Belloc at the time no intention of marrying, but he learnt, though he kept them to himself, certain facts which were much to the lady's discredit. Further, their acquaintance, always slight, had ended some time before he had met Louise Swanton.

As Colonel Swanton would not allow his daughter to see her future husband without a third person being present—this being the usual procedure with regard to every French betrothal—Mary Clarke had perforce to act as intermediary. But Louise still felt unhappy and undecided; and Mary, feeling certain her friend's happiness depended on the marriage, persuaded her to meet Hilaire in Mrs. Clarke's house. During their interview Hilaire convinced Louise she was the only woman who had ever touched his imagination, and that she had indeed won what many occurrences in his long life prove to have been a singularly noble and selfless heart.

I think it likely Adelaide de Montgolfier remained unaware of this episode, for my grandmother was a most reserved woman, and in her letters I have seldom found any reference to herself, and hardly ever even a passing allusion to her past life. But whether or not Mademoiselle knew of how greatly indebted her friend had reason to be to Mary Clarke, she evidently made up her mind to break the tie between the two young women, and, as often happens in such a case, Miss Clarke unwittingly played into the hand of her enemy.

She came one day to see Madame Swanton Belloc, who had lately been confined. Adelaide de Montgolfier came out of the invalid's room, and said curtly, "Louise is not feeling well, and does not wish to see you." Mary, filled with anger, and feeling deeply hurt, wrote Louise a note in which she said, "It must be either Adelaide or me." And when Louise answered, pointing out how unreasonable was this ultimatum, the other broke off all relations between herself and the Bellocs.

From every point of view this break was a great misfortune to one of the two women. Not only did my grandmother lose a devoted friend—but after Mary Clarke's marriage all the noted

Englishmen and Englishwomen who came to Paris, brought an introduction to the now celebrated *salonnière* of the rue du Bac. Had their friendship pursued a normal course, the pleasure and mental change Mary Clarke had brought into Louise Swanton's youth woud have continued all through what became, if a full and happy life, yet one often burdened with care and anxiety.

Yet under the ashes of that seemingly long-dead relationship remained living embers. In one of the lives of Madame Mohl it is stated that before Hilaire Belloc's death, a reconciliation took place, and that "the three old friends would meet and talk over old times." I am convinced this is untrue, for my grandfather had bitterly resented Mary Clarke's conduct to his wife, and the Bellocs are not a forgiving clan. More conclusive is the fact that "the three old friends" could not have met, except in the presence of Adelaide de Montgolfier, who in Paris was constantly, indeed daily, in and out of the Belloc's *appartement*, and who spent each summer in their country house. Mademoiselle's hatred of her one-time rival had increased as the years went on, for she believed, what I am inclined to think was true, that Madame Mohl now and again would speak of her as deformed. She is so described in both the long biographies written of this noted lady. One of Mademoiselle's shoulders was slightly higher than the other, but as she wore a little pad on the lower shoulder, this was not notice-able.

What is certainly true is that immediately after the death of Hilaire Belloc, in the autumn of 1866, Madame Mohl made a tentative effort to effect a reconciliation with his widow. But Madame Swanton Belloc was not only extremely unhappy, she had become seriously ill. Also, her three children were distressed and offended by an action which, though no doubt done with a kind intention, was surely ill-advised.

During the two years which preceded his death, Hilaire Belloc was very infirm, and lived entirely at La Celle Saint Cloud. But he had shrunk from giving up his studio, and it still contained a number of unfinished paintings and drawings.

When came his death, which seems to have struck every member of his family with surprise, as well as great distress, his widow, their son, and younger daughter, Lily Ballot, wished to empty the studio, and destroy its contents. But to this his elder daughter, Louise Redelsperger, who generally raised objections to what those about her desired should be done, strongly demurred, and at her suggestion it was arranged a sale should be held there. Unfortunately, this became known to Madame Mohl. She attended the sale, bought a number of the unfinished paintings and sketches, and herself took them to the rue de l'École de Médecine. My grandmother was too ill to be told of these gifts, but Louise Redelsperger, furious at what had happened, no doubt all the more as it was, in a sense, her fault, at once called on Madame Mohl and insisted on paying her what she had spent. The drawings so acquired were given to some of Hilaire Belloc's old pupils in the art school of which he had been head for thirty-two years.

Madame Swanton Belloc's illness lasted for nearly two months; but when she was well again, and learned of Madame Mohl's kind thought, she wrote her a grateful note. In that note she incidentally explained that she and her son were anxious to let the smaller of their two houses at La Celle Saint Cloud.

Early in that spring (1867) two Englishwomen, Bessie Parkes and Barbara Bodichon, wished to spend a few weeks near Paris. Madame Mohl told them the châlet Belloc was to let; and thus, by a most singular chance, it came about that she played a part in the marriage of my parents even more decisive than that she had played, nearly fifty years before, in the marriage of the Hilaire Bellocs. My mother ever after felt, and once warmly expressed for her in a letter, a feeling of affection and of gratitude.

During my childhood, Mary Mohl paid fairly frequent visits to our French home. By that time her husband had died, and when feeling lonely, she would now and again suddenly propose coming to La Celle Saint Cloud for a few days. Her visit always upset the quiet household, for she did not bring a maid, and she had all sorts of odd ideas with regard to food, and the way daily life should be conducted. So my mother gradually came to realize how very different was Madame Mohl from the kind of woman she was supposed to be by her London friends, for it was impossible for her to pose, or show any of the affectations some of these same friends found so delightful, in Madame Swanton Belloc's presence. She was the only visitor of whom I, as a child, felt afraid. I dimly apprehended her jealousy, even of my mother, and I shrank from the obvious satisfaction felt by her in seeing the melancholy state into which had fallen her old enemy, the poor little lady my brother and I had been taught to love and reverence under the name of Maman-Aïde.

To return to the years when Adelaide de Montgolfier played so great a part in the life of the friend she loved with so possessive a love. She was on good terms with Hilaire Belloc, and each enjoyed the other's cleverness and wit; but my aunts, Lily and Louise, strangely different as they were the one from the other, much resented Mademoiselle's constant presence. And they had good reason for their resentment, for she persistently tried to interfere in their upbringing and education. Fortunately for them both, she failed in these endeavours, for their parents had definite views, which were transmitted to both their granddaughters, that is myself and Juliette Siry. Those views are that daughters should be allowed as far as possible to go their own way, and not have their brains over-burdened with what was later to be called the higher education.

All the same, as the sisters, each in her turn, grew into womanhood, their feelings of resentment became intensified, for Mademoiselle considered she had a right to try and promote their settlement in life. Here, again, her wishes were disregarded, and completely thwarted by the young women concerned. They both chose their own husbands, and in both cases their mother's friend strongly disapproved of their choice.

Even so, as the years went on, Lily and Louise were both too intelligent and kind-hearted not to feel touched by the affection Adelaide de Montgolfier had always showed them; and a kinder feeling grew up between them and Mademoiselle. As to their brother, the relationship of Louis Belloc with his godmother was cloudless throughout the whole of his forty-two years of life. He loved her tenderly, and on the day of his marriage he spoke of her to my mother with strong feeling, and expressed a hope his wife would try both to love and to understand her.

During the Siege of Paris, Aunt Lily and her husband, Charles Ballot, saw Mademoiselle constantly, and they greatly admired her extraordinary pluck, and the way she faced up to the difficult conditions of life in the beleaguered city. At one time they actually suggested she should go and live with them, but she firmly refused even to think of doing so. Though she was then eighty-three, she was more like a vigorous woman of sixty, and she always walked from the *Quartier Latin,* to where the Ballots lived in the Place de la Concorde, two or three times a week.

No balloon ever left Paris for England without bearing a letter from Adelaide de Montgolfier to my grandmother, who was then living with her elder daughter at Richmond. This one-sided correspondence was indeed a proof of faithful love, for no letter from England reached Paris during the Siege.

After my father's death, when Mademoiselle fell into the piteous condition I have described, though she went on living in her own *appartement,* some member of our family went to see her every day, and Lily Ballot showed her the most tender and devoted care. Her curious mental state must have darkened the last years of my grandmother's life, and when they were togther at La Celle Saint Cloud (for Maman-Aïde went on spending each summer there) Madame Swanton Belloc, her face filled with pain, would sit gazing at her poor old friend.

Though she was ninety-three, Mademoiselle's death took every one by surprise, for her mother had lived to be over a hundred. Also, she had not gone downhill, as do almost all old people. She had remained exactly the same. Then, one day in the winter of 1880, my mother received from Aunt Lily the following letter:

"I wonder if you will be surprised, my darling, to learn that the children's poor Maman-Aïde has gone to a world which, whatever it be like, will be to her filled with radiant joy, because she will there find my brother Louis.

"Her maid sent word that my godmother did not feel well; so I went and spent the night sitting by her bed. She died in a moment, as if she had been a child falling asleep on her mother's breast. My sister Louise came at once, and was extremely kind, taking on herself all the painful details which follow, with us, on every death. Meanwhile, Charles occupied himself with sending many telegrams to members of the de Mongolfier and de Canson families.

"As you will readily believe, my mother took the news quietly, and made no comment. Although she did not say so, I know it must have been a relief."

Adelaide de Montgolfier left all she possessed to Lily Ballot. But my aunt refused the legacy, and I lately read her reason for this decision:

"To me the sum in question would have been a fortune. But when I examined my conscience, I felt it would be wrong that after having taken all her life, a member of our family should take all her money as well. God alone knows whether I was right or wrong, and I will tell you what I have told no one else. I went through a bitter struggle, thinking of what a difference it would make not only to my husband, but to my dear son, Marcel. However, I need hardly tell you that Charles said not a word to influence me, neither did my mother, though I think they both thought that I was perhaps too scrupulous as, though the relations whom I hope will ultimately benefit by this reversion are ill off, certain members of her family are, as we know, extremely rich.

"All this my dear, my beloved sister, is for you alone. I mean by that—say nothing of it to our mother when you see her."

I think my aunt was partly influenced in her decision because she was aware that during the greater part of her life she had disliked her godmother.

IV

IN mid August there arrived, addressed to my mother, a letter which was to bring me new friendships and interests, and which profoundly affected, and still affects, my life.

A sheet of thin notepaper, headed with the one engraved word *Croissy*, lies before me. The sloping handwriting in which the following, signed Jeanne Déroulède, is written, has about it something childish and unformed:

"I am writing on behalf of my mother, who thinks you must have heard of her from Madame Swanton Belloc, for whom she cherished a deep devotion.

"We have learnt that you are at La Celle St. Cloud, and my mother is exceedingly anxious to make your acquaintance and that of your daughter. Her state of health makes it impossible for her to come and see you, as she would naturally have wished to do, and, as this is impossible, she hopes you will have the kindness to come and dine with us next Sunday."

We had neither of us ever heard the name of Déroulède. But everything connected with Madame Swanton Belloc was dear to us both, and the only people my mother now enjoyed seeing when we were in France, were those who had been in any way connected with the lives of Hilaire Belloc and his wife. She therefore accepted the invitation, and sent the letter to her sister-in-law, Lily Ballot, from whom it brought the following reply:

"When I read the letter you sent me, I was filled with an immense surprise. It was like a voice echoing down the corridors of a distant past.

"I cannot help thinking that Maman must have spoken to you of Amélie Déroulède, for there was no younger woman for whom she felt a greater affection and, before you see her, I feel you ought to know the following facts.

"Amélie is a sister of our great playwright, Émile Augier. Her parents were living at La Celle St. Cloud when my parents first went there about the year 1830, and Amélie, who was ravishingly beautiful, from childhood, experienced a veritable cult for Maman. After she married, she belonged to a brilliant world, partly composed of those whose lives centre in the theatre, and partly in the society which then clustered round the Court. Even so, she constantly came to our house at times she thought she would find our mother alone.

"As you know, my dear sister, I have always delighted in beauty, and so it was always a pleasure to me to catch a fleeting glimpse of that exquisite creature. She was tall, her features were perfect, and she had masses of fair hair which she wore somewhat fantastically arranged. I knew nothing of her private life, except that rumour credited her with having many adorers who, my mother believed, sighed in vain.

"Maman, who was grieved I did not insist on associating with this devoted younger friend of hers, would tell me now and again of how passionate was Amélie's love for her two sons, André and Paul. When those two boys were just grown up, to the great surprise of those about her, their mother produced a little daughter, who must be rather older than our Marie.

"I do not remember when Amélie became a widow; but I think it must have been before that tragic summer of 1870 you and I remember so well. Paul and André Déroulède at once joined the army, and a month later came the frightful tidings that they had

both been killed at the battle of Sédan.

"The effect on their mother was catastrophic. She had a stroke, followed by a terrible illness; and she was still supposed to be in danger of death, when came the news that her sons were prisoners of war in Germany. Paul Déroulède refused to give his word that he would not try to escape, and escape he did. His brother, who was three or four years younger than he, stayed at Coblentz until peace was signed.

"But relief from sorrow does not put back the clock. Amélie became entirely paralysed, and ever since then she has refused to see even her closest friends. She would not even see my mother, who had meant so much to her, and who all her life had been, I believe, the only woman she had ever loved. So she has lived, for fifteen years, a kind of death in life, in a villa at Croissy. The house overlooks the Seine, and is next door to the country-house of her brother, Émile Augier. One shrinks from contemplating the suffering she must inflict on her daughter in forcing the girl to lead a life so mournful and so unnatural. Jeanne Déroulède never leaves Croissy, excepting when her aunt, Madame Guiard, who also has a house at Croissy, takes her to Paris for the day. Meanwhile Améile's whole life is said to centre round her elder son.

"You are so fond of reading the newspapers that you surely know something of that extraordinary man, Paul Déroulède? But I doubt if you are aware that not long after the war, he published a small volume of verse called *Chants du Soldat*. The book was commended at a special session of the Academy, and it is said to have sold, in the last few years, more than Béranger's verses have done in fifty years. Yet, instead of following in his uncle's footsteps, or pursuing some useful profession, this modern Don Quixote has given up his whole life to what hotheads call *La Revanche*. With a view to bringing this about, not long ago he founded what he chooses to call the Patriots' League. It is said

to contain something like half a million members. My son René has Déroulède in horror, and regards him as a most dangerous element in our public life. While calling himself a Republican, he hates and despises the Government, though he cannot suggest, or so René declares, anything to put in its place. He spends his time going all over the country preaching a doctrine of hate for Germany, so I do not think you are likely to meet him at Croissy.

"No doubt what inspired Amélie with a desire to see you, is owing to her sister or brother having heard that Marie is considered very like our mother. In any case the dear child may be able to do something to brighten the life of the unfortunate daughter."

After having read my aunt's letter, I formed in my mind a picture of Jeanne Déroulède. I saw her as sickly-looking, limited in mind, and in every way unlike the girls I now met daily at La Celle Saint Cloud. As I had in those days what is called in France "a good little heart," I fervently hoped her mother would allow her to come to some of the gatherings of young people who were now bringing so much pleasure and amusement into my life.

We were compelled to watch every *sou* we spent, so my mother settled we should walk the three miles to Croissy. But she arranged for us to be called for after dinner, by a man willing to drive us back in an old victoria for the reasonable fee of three francs.

The then little town of Bougival formed my boundary in that beloved countryside, and though I now feel how odd it should have been so, I had never crossed the bridge which led to the island on which was built the still small town of Croissy. But my mother had the liking for maps she transmitted to my brother, and she soon found on her map of Seine-et-Oise the riverside road, a considerable distance from Croissy, where Madame Dé-

MARIE BELLOC
at the age of twenty

roulède's villa, if it overlooked the Seine, must be. So after crossing the bridge, we turned sharp to the left, where was a carriage-
way which might have been a hundred miles from Paris. On one
side was a stretch of meadowland, on the other flowed the river
and, after a while, we saw a large house, set in a formal garden,
which had about it an air of smug prosperity.

We walked on, and I suddenly espied a tall girl standing in the
middle of the road. I at once guessed the girl to be Jeanne Déroulède; and as I hurried towards her, I gazed at her with astonishment, so completely different was she to what I had imagined
her.

Jeanne had not inherited her mother's beauty, with the exception of masses of *blond cendré* hair which she wore thrown
back from her forehead, and she had irregular, strongly-marked,
features. But she possessed what is rather rare among Frenchwomen, a brilliant complexion, and her large blue eyes were full
of challenge and of gaiety. She greeted us warmly, and swinging
open a gate, led us through a not over-tidy garden to a widely-
opened french window. *"Les voilà!"* she called out, in a joyous
eager voice.

I walked up into a sitting-room, and during a few moments,
coming in from the bright sunlight of a mid-August afternoon,
I saw nothing. Then, gradually, I became aware that opposite
the widely-open window was a long narrow couch, placed as
though it were a catafalque, in the centre of the room.

On that couch the immobile figure of Madame Déroulède lay
stretched out, her head resting on high pillows covered with some
kind of dark silk. Her still lovely oval face was rouged, and
framed in large curls which were thickly powdered. Far her most
arresting feature were her blue-green widely-opened eyes which,
as I was soon to know, were capable of expressing an extraordinary range of feeling. She wore, that day, a gown made of thin
violet-coloured silk, and draping her shoulders was an old lace

{ 41 }

shawl. Her figure, seeming unnaturally long, was set in a singular kind of trembling immobility.

Her speech was extremely indistinct, and I think only three people, when she spoke, really understood what she was trying to express. The one was a maid who had been with her since the beginning of her illness, and the other two her daughter Jeanne and her son Paul. They were all able to interpret at once what she wished to convey. Her brain was quite clear, her mind brilliant and acute, and she was keenly interested in everything happening in the worlds of politics and literature.

On that first evening I was asked to sit down close to her, and she murmured something which Jeanne translated as being that I was indeed very like Madame Swanton Belloc. This supposed likeness was certainly heightened by the fact that I wore my hair parted in the middle, which in those days was regarded as ugly and eccentric. She asked certain questions about my brother, who was then in England staying with a school friend, and she then added something, which touched my mother, concerning my father. This was she had known Louis very well in his early life, when she used frequently to go and see his mother, and that his delicacy of heart and kindness of nature recalled his father, Monsieur Belloc.

After a time, a double door to the left of the couch was thrown open, showing a room where was a dining-table laid for four; and Jeanne cried out eagerly that now we were going to meet her brother.

Though she was very fond of André, Paul was her hero, and he soon became, and remained, my hero too.

When I first saw him, Paul Déroulède was thirty-nine, and unlike any Frenchman I had ever seen. He was exceptionally tall, had a shock of fair hair, and his strongly marked features and large nose made him an easy subject for caricature. Like his sister, he had a delightful, unforced, easily aroused sense of humour.

He never spoke of himself, or betrayed any knowledge of the position he had achieved among hundreds of thousands of his fellow countrymen. But among those hundreds of thousands, there was not even one distinguished contemporary. Yet I think it can be truly said that had he lived to even extreme old age, the collapse of France in 1940 would not have happened.

No life has been written of Paul Déroulède, and this emboldens me to try and give what must remain an inadequate account of the noblest and most selfless man I have ever known. And let me say, by way of preamble, that perhaps Déroulède's most unusual trait was his magnanimity.

During my now long life I have known a certain number of men who played a considerable part in the public life of whatever happened to be their country. But I have only known three men who possessed that rarest of qualities. Those three men were Paul Déroulède, Henry Asquith, and Edward Grey of Fallodon. I never heard one of these three utter a word of blame, or what would have been in every case more justified, of contempt, of any opponent who had assailed them—and that even when the attack had been made much below the belt.

Edward Grey, unlike Henry Asquith, seldom talked of men and women, but I recall hearing him once utter a few words of strong admiration for the outstanding courage and energy, shown in some crucial circumstance, by the one man who had been his enemy throughout the whole war of 1914–18 and, indeed, long after the war had ended. As for Mr. Asquith, I saw him fairly frequently, in triumph and in defeat. Even then I thought I knew a great deal concerning the meaner side of human nature, but I was amazed at the way certain people, far more men than women, treated that really great Englishman after what, I suppose, must be called his fall. But I never heard from him a word of recrimination.

But note the difference in the public lives of the three men

I have now in mind.

During their more strenuous and difficult years of service to their country, Asquith and Grey were supported by the complete confidence—I think it is true to say—of millions of their fellow countrymen and countrywomen. Each of them was also blessed with devoted personal friends in whose eyes they could do no wrong. Asquith enjoyed an exceedingly happy family life, and was most fortunate in his children. Not only were they in their different ways brilliant and successful, they gave him all their love and confidence.

Grey was also exceptionally fortunate in his friends, and men and women belonging to quite different types of human nature felt for him, and showed him, profound affection. As was the case with Asquith, he had two periods of exceedingly happy home life, though those nearest to him were aware of how he had longed to have children.

Compare the lot of these two Englishmen with that of Paul Déroulède? From when he escaped from a German prison camp to France at the age of twenty-five, this Frenchman, born in a world where, with the one tragic interlude of the Franco-Prussian War, it only depended on himself to enjoy every kind of personal and material success, gave up the whole of his life, and of what money he had, to the onerous task of keeping alight what had become in his country a thin and flickering flame of patriotism.

That flame he not only kept alive, but caused to burn more and more brightly for forty-four years, in the face of strong official opposition, and the often angry disapproval of all those belonging to what must be called, for want of a better term, his own class. By all the educated Frenchmen of his day he was regarded as a dangerous crank who desired to embroil his country with a neighbour whose one wish was to live with her in amity and peace. The kinder of his critics considered him, as my aunt had written to my mother, as the arch type of tiresome idealist

who spends an idle life tilting at windmills. He was naturally loathed, as well as feared, by the venal politicians who knew they had in him a watchful and implacable enemy. He was even looked at askance by the chiefs of the French Army, then still smarting from the knowledge that the professional soldiers had been found wanting in the summer of 1870. When Déroulède was mentioned in the Paris press, which was seldom, the mention always took the form of an attack, and always the attack was made in contemptuous terms.

In a brilliant biography, published since the last war, of an Englishman who was the most successful British ambassador of his day, the biographer observes, concerning Bismarck's policy: "He believed, and rightly, in the French desire for revenge." Now, in my view, though I have no doubt that this assertion as regards Bismarck's belief was correct, all those who lived in the France of the eighties and nineties of the last century could not but be aware, if they gave the matter any thought, the French had less than any desire for revenge. I was fairly often in Paris between our first return to La Celle Saint Cloud, in 1885, and my marriage in 1896, and during those years I saw and talked to men and women belonging to every class of Frenchmen and Frenchwomen. From the drivers of the Paris *fiacres* to the many people I met at the houses of my relations, and friends in the French literary world, I do not recall a single human being, with the exception of Paul Déroulède, who believed in the possibility of another Franco-Prussian war. Once a year a gathering of men and women took place below the shrouded statue of Strassburg, in the Place de la Concorde; but it was almost entirely composed of Alsatians and Lorrainers who lived in Paris. The one desire of the France of those days was to be left to live in peace. Here and there some intelligent man—I never heard a woman except my mother say so—would express a fear that Germany was not sated; but that expression of fear was never coupled with any

wish to regain the lost provinces.

Paul Déroulède's delightful human qualities caused him to be held in affection by his uncle, Émile Augier, and by Madame Déroulède's sister. Only his mother and Jeanne approved of the work to which he was dedicating his life, and none of his relations—no other people, excepting ourselves, ever came to Madame Déroulède's house—even made fleeting allusions to the *Ligue des Patriotes*. Yet that vast association was naturally known to absorb all his time and thoughts. He accepted this heartless boycott with easy good-humour, as being quite natural, and he spent every moment he could spare at Croissy so as to be with the mother he loved with a rarely expressed devotion. All the same, I know, now, that one reason why Madame Déroulède and Jeanne became so fondly attached to me was because I, too, found myself in full sympathy with Paul's views, and believed, as did my mother, that another Franco-Prussian war was inevitable.

I never heard Paul allude to his famous *Chants du Soldat;* but he had specially bound, no doubt at his mother's suggestion, a copy of the little book of verse; and one Sunday night, after we had finished dinner, and were sitting round the couch of Madame Déroulède, he pushed it into my hand. At once Madame Déroulède murmured something to Jeanne, and Jeanne said their mother wished him to read aloud to Madame Louis Belloc her favourite among his poems.

I held out the book, and he read, in a quiet, unemotional voice, the noble verses of which I give the concluding lines:

> Et la chanson dit vrai, tant pis pour qui la raille;
> Mourir pour la patrie est le sort le plus beau!
> Et si je dois tomber en un jour de bataille,
> C'est au sol Prussien que je veux mon tombeau.

Concerning much of what he was doing during that first stage of my acquaintance with these dear friends was told me at odd

times by his sister, for he himself never spoke of it, and I never heard him allude to Germany.

The only thing which affected him was an assault on his personal honour, and during the first twenty years of what might be called his working life, he fought several duels. With regard to one of these duels occurred the following curious circumstance.

Our friendship with the Déroulèdes provided interest and amusement at La Celle Saint Cloud. My cousins were all attached to my mother, but they regarded her as an incurably romantic idealist, and her knowledge of, and interest in, the French republican world of that day surprised and puzzled them.

Étienne Siry used to bring back each evening from Paris all kinds of news, and I remember his saying one evening at dinner that Aunt Bessie's new friend, Paul Déroulède, had just had a violent altercation with one of his political opponents, and that they were going to fight a duel. Some days later I learned the following strange story.

Both the quarrel and the coming duel had been carefully kept from Madame Déroulède. Jeanne used to read the papers to her every day, and it was naturally easy to prevent her learning anything those about her did not wish should come to her knowledge. But the moving French saying, attributed to Madame Victor Hugo, *"Dieu s'est dit, 'Je ne peux pas être partout,' et Il créa la mère,"* certainly applied to this mother.

On the morning the duel had taken place, a carriage drove up to the gate. Jeanne stood up, commanding herself and her nerves completely, while waiting for the bearer of either good or bad news, when suddenly Madame Déroulède who, since her daughter had been a little child, had apparently been incapable of moving, rose from her couch, and walked steadily across to the open window. Paul, hurrying up the garden, was just in time to catch her in his arms before she fell.

He had wounded his assailant, but the man would be all right

after a few weeks in bed. So all was well.

Although he never alluded to the part he himself was playing in the life of his country, he and my mother would sometimes engage in an eager political discussion. He had a fierce contempt for the then French parliamentary system. All he wanted in its place was some decent form of government. I remember his telling us that in ten years there had been two hundred French cabinet ministers, and that it was common knowledge the majority of deputies allowed their votes to be influenced by the hope each had of becoming a minister. That Déroulède professed himself a strong Republican, while violently disapproving of the statesmen and politicians who formed the Republic of his day, much irritated the Bonapartists and Legitimists, who would have welcomed him into their fold. Certain men among them, at least, felt France ought to be prepared to face a possible war.

Now and again a paragraph mentioning Déroulède would appear in some English newspaper. One such, which I read with amusement, described how this chauvinist had recently bought a plot of land at Croissy, where he had built, as a speculation, a number of houses, one of which he had the luck to let to the well-known dramatist, Émile Augier. I never saw written by the Paris correspondent of a London paper any allusion to the *Ligue des Patriotes*, or to even one of the innumerable meetings Paul was holding all over his country, and that though he was pro-British at a time England was not liked or trusted in France. Gladstone's attitude during the war of 1870–71 was still remembered, and Queen Victoria was regarded as strongly pro-German, though the French, with their logical minds, regarded this as natural, as her daughter was the future German Empress.

A certain sensation was caused when, just after the then prominent French statesman, Jules Ferry, had suggested the formation of a kind of loose alliance with Germany, Paul Déroulède, in a public speech, pointed out that any such understanding would

really be an alliance directed against England, and debar the English from playing any part if, and when, Germany again attacked France. This speech was not quoted in the British press; yet it was the only one of Déroulède's public utterances which did affect the policy of the French Government. The then President of the French Republic received thousands of letters reminding him of how the Germans had behaved during the Franco-Prussian War, and Ferry was told to forget his ill-advised suggestion.

On another occasion it was as if Déroulède foresaw what happened in 1940, for he wrote:

"Invasion is not defeat. In 1870 we allowed our military movements to be dictated by political considerations, and fell back on Paris when we should have stood our ground. If our country ever does this again, we shall lose the war."

That summer my cousin, René Millet, was passing through Paris, and came to spend the day at La Celle Saint Cloud. He had written and told my mother that after lunching with Juliette Siry he would come and see us. By that time he was the most important of the younger men in our family, and was already a distinguished diplomat. He had been my father's best man, and he was my godfather. Though with me affection was tempered by fear, for he held certain views as to the education and bringing-up of girls with which I did not at all agree, his constant kindness, and the love he had showed me from my earliest childhood, made me truly fond of him.

He came later than we had thought he would do, and I had an afternoon engagement. But he asked me to give up going out, as he had something important to say he thought I ought to hear.

I can see the scene now. My mother and I sitting in the *grand salon* near the wide-open windows, and René standing before us. He was tall, and looked more like an Englishman than a

Frenchman, the more so that he had a lean, taut face.

He began by saying that he had learned from his mother that we were often at Croissy; and he explained that after giving the matter some thought, he had made up his mind to beg my mother not to take her son there. He pointed out that Hilaire, then aged fifteen, was at an impressionable age, and that it would be a most unfortunate thing if Paul Déroulède obtained any influence over him. And then he gave us a picture of the European situation as he saw it.

He started by excusing himself, for he was always courteous, indeed punctilious, for wishing to say certain things, as he felt sure his Aunt Bessie knew all the facts as well, if not better, than he did. She might not, however, have given to those facts the serious thought he was naturally compelled to do.

He reminded her that two old men were now ruling Germany —the one, the Emperor, not far off ninety; the other, Bismarck, a tiger whose teeth had been drawn. Both these old men wished for peace, and desired to live on good terms with France. The Crown Prince, whose accession could not long be delayed, given his father's age, was a liberal and enlightened man, strongly under the influence of his wife, who had always remained "the Englishwoman," and believed in constitutional government. Thus Paul Déroulède's conviction the Germans would in time provoke another war was not only nonsense, but extremely dangerous nonsense.

My mother intervened, and recalled how very nearly Germany had fallen again on France, meaning to finish her once and for all, within a few years of the Franco-Prussian War. She said she had been told by the then Dean of Westminster, Arthur Stanley, that this plan, or plot, had been divulged to Queen Victoria, who had written to the Czar begging him to intervene.

I remember, over all these years, how annoyed René became at this interruption. He brushed it aside, though he must have known what my mother said was true. But over ten years had gone by since it had happened.

Returning to Déroulède, he said that the *Ligue des Patriotes* was a dangerous association, which was giving a good deal of trouble to the Government. As to Alsace and Lorraine being ever restored to France, it was a crazy dream, and would never come to pass; and again and again he reiterated his fear lest my brother should fall under so dangerous an influence as that of Paul Déroulède.

I had remained silent while René was expounding his views. He was used to a considerable measure of deference, and was accustomed to his opinion being taken. But my mother, to my secret joy, stood up to him. She pointed out that Hilaire was being entirely educated in England, under the care of Cardinal Newman, and so was very little in France. As to Paul Déroulède, she expressed her admiration for his character, and said that no Frenchman she had met had ever impressed her with such a sense of his high-mindedness and sincerity of purpose. She admitted, however, that she knew very little of his political activities, as he never mentioned them in his mother's house when guests were present. She further expressed her opinion of how very unfortunate she thought it that Frenchmen of good-will did not play a greater part in the politics of their country. As to that René agreed, for he much admired the manner in which British public life was then conducted.

He ended by expressing his pleasure at the fact that owing to our unfortunate friendship with the Déroulèdes, I had the great privilege of meeting now and again Émile Augier, the greatest playwright since Molière. He further said he hoped his dear little god-daughter listened carefully to everything Monsieur Augier said, as the slightest utterance of such a man would be of value, and should be of the greatest interest, to any young person.

V

MY godfather's warnings and admonitions did not affect our friendship with the Déroulèdes, and we dined with them at least once a week all that summer and autumn.

I think it must have been after our third Sunday dinner at Croissy, that Madame Déroulède murmured something to her daughter, while there trembled over her mouth the half-smile which now and again would quiver there. Jeanne reddened, and then she said her mother wished us to know that Monsieur and Madame Augier were coming in to see us. She added that her Uncle Émile, as a young man, had been very fond of my grandparents.

What Madame Déroulède had really said was, "Here come Philemon and Baucis" (the French equivalent of Darby and Joan). I know this because, after the Augiers had come and gone, Émile Augier's sister insisted on Jeanne repeating exactly what it was she had said.

A few moments later there came in from the garden a tall, burly, elderly man, accompanied by a tiny little lady who looked much older than he did. I was vaguely aware that Émile Augier was considered to be the greatest playwright of his day; but I had never been to one of his plays. Going to the theatre would have involved spending a night in a Paris hotel, and expenses which my mother would have thought it wrong to incur.

There echoes in my ears, after more than fifty years, the sound of Monsieur Augier's authoritative voice, and the perfectly balanced, eloquent French he always spoke. Expressing warm pleasure at meeting us, he produced a little book for children which he said had been given to him by Maria Edgeworth during a visit she had made to the château of La Celle Saint Cloud forty to fifty years before, and which he had brought to give me.

He seemed so commonplace, compared with Madame Déroulède and her son, that I felt vaguely disappointed. But soon a time came when I never saw Émile Augier, and we saw him often in his sister's house, without feeling a thrill of romantic interest in his personality.

Even on that first occasion I was touched by the affection and deference which the famous man, in those days regarded as a very famous man—showed his wife. To this day I do not know her Christian name, for he always called her by the sentimental old appellation of "m'amie"; and the next time we lunched in Paris with Aunt Lily, she told my mother the moving story of these two people's lives.

Augier had enjoyed, when still a very young man, a taste of real glory with his first slight comedy; and during the twenty years that followed he constantly won the palm without the dust. He was devoted, as only a Frenchman seems able to be, not only to the widowed mother with whom he went on living, but also to his two married sisters. But quite soon, when their Émile was twenty-six, across these three women's lives swept a deep shadow. They learnt he had fallen deeply in love with a young actress, of no great beauty, then acting in one of his plays, and soon he told his mother he intended to make her his wife. Madame Augier wrote him a formal letter, for she could not trust herself to speak of the matter, in which she declared she would rather die in torment than give her consent to what she would consider so disastrous a marriage. As for his sisters, they felt certain his passion for the girl—she was only nineteen—would soon die down.

Now according to French law, and as far as I know it has not been altered, every French parent has a complete right of veto regarding the marriage of any of his or her children. But there exists a way of defeating this Draconian law. The son or daughter is open to undertake what are called *sommations respectueuses*. The young man (I have never heard of this step being taken by a woman), accompanied by his lawyer, pays a formal call on each of his parents, and summons them to allow his marriage to take place. This interview occurs every three months, and in my youth the process took a year. At the end of the year, the marriage can be solemnized. I know of one case where every time the *sommation respectueuse* took place, the mother threw herself on the floor, and kneeling before her son, implored him to give up doing that which she believed would lead to the ruin of his life.

Émile Augier, as indeed all those familiar with his dramatic work will readily apprehend, had the greatest respect for what the French call by the generic term of *la famille*. Further, he loved his mother so dearly he did not feel he could bring himself to subject her to what she would regard as such an ignominy as would have been these legal proceedings. But he did not give up the girl he loved, and who loved him. What he did do was to exact of her what I think was a most cruel price, and she consented to pay it. It took the form that she should leave the stage and live a retired life, never seeing any man but himself, or any friend of his he chose to introduce to her.

His fame grew ever greater and, as the years went on, his mother and sisters made many attempts to induce him to make what they would have regarded as a suitable marriage. But they failed completely. In time, though his mother did not weaken, Amélie Déroulède and his other sister, Madame Guiard, consented to become acquainted with the lady of his heart, and, after he had built a villa at Croissy, she used to spend each summer with him there. She was a middle-aged woman when her lover's mother died, at last, in extreme old age, and their marriage duly took place.

Madame Émile Augier dressed in a very quiet old-fashioned way, and though she was younger by some years, she appeared far older than either of her sisters-in-law. We asked her several times to come to La Celle Saint Cloud, but she never did so, though she always seemed genuinely pleased to see us.

When we paid what I think was our only call on her, while Monsieur Augier and my mother were talking together, Madame Augier took me into her garden. She said she had been much interested in meeting me, as Madame Déroulède had told her I bore so strong a resemblance to Madame Swanton Belloc. She added she used to often hear of my grandmother, and knew how much not only Amélie, but Émile, also, cared for her, so she had longed for an opportunity to know her and to care for her too, but that circumstances had made this impossible.

What his wife said to me that day concerning her husband's affection for Madame Swanton Belloc was proved to be true not long ago, when I found a letter of Émile Augier. Simply dated "Friday," it was obviously written in answer to an inquiry, made in 1873, as to his sister's illness. It ended with the hope that Madame Swanton Belloc would believe in the expression of a tender affection which, though they now seldom met, would ever remain living in his heart.

All my relations envied my ever-growing closer acquaintance with the famous dramatist, and I was taken, as a special treat, by Aunt Lily and Uncle Charles, to see the most popular of his plays, *Le Gendre de Monsieur Poirier*. But though I enjoyed it, I had even then seen plays which had given me far more pleasure.

Although Émile Augier is seldom mentioned in contemporary dramatic French literature, innumerable fellow countrymen and fellow countrywomen of his often quote some telling line from one of his plays. Several popular French sayings come from *Le*

Gendre de Monsieur Poirier, and the last time I was in Paris a working woman told me of a couple who thought the time had come when they could afford themselves *"le luxe d'un garçon."*

To my thinking, Augier deserves a better fate than that which has befallen him, for he was the first European playwright who went straight to human nature for his models, and his plays almost always dealt with the stuff of which average human nature is made. He was fortunate inasmuch as the romantics had gone out of fashion—even the mighty Victor Hugo's dramas were laughed at in the fifties and sixties of the last century—and the naturalists, from Balzac to Flaubert, had not written for the theatre. So the field, for a whole generation, was open to such a playwright as he at once proved himself to be.

As was strikingly shown in the matter of his marriage, he was a man of determined character and will. This was proved by what he did when still apparently at the height not only of his fame, but of his power. To the incredulous astonishment of his family, his friends, and of the public, he suddenly gave up play-writing. He never offered any public explanation of this strange decision. But he told a younger friend, who told me, one of the reasons. Just before the first night of what was to be his last play, he happened to be in the study of the then Director of the Comédie Française, when a card was brought in. The Director looked at it; frowned; smiled; and then exclaimed, "I won't see him! Say I'm out! I do wish the old devil would leave me in peace."

He threw the card on the table, and Augier saw that on it was inscribed *Eugène Scribe.* Now Scribe had been the most successful dramatist of his time, and so, for years, master of the French theatre. The then great Augier said to himself, "That shall never happen to me."

Though the France of his day has altered more than has any other country in Europe in, say, the last eighty years, Augier's sense of character makes, even now, his plays memorable; and those who wish to know what French society, in a broad sense, was like in the sixties and seventies of the last century, will find no better source of information. Always he went his own independent way, and I once heard him allude with satisfaction to the fact that *Les Lionnes Pauvres* so alarmed the censor that he, the author, was compelled to make many severe cuts. In 1876 he shocked his faithful public by producing a play which was, in effect, a plea for divorce.

I should like to stress what I think cannot but prove of interest to every thoughtful mind, at the present time of the world's history. This man, who held so honoured a place in the imagination of practically every educated Frenchman, stood completely aside from everything that had to do with the government of his country. Though he had no sympathy with his nephew, Paul Déroulède's, passionate wish to revive militant patriotism in their nation, he shared Paul's contempt of politicians of every kind and type. He may have been, in a tepid way, an Imperialist, for he had been a welcome guest at the Tuileries, though in no sense as welcome as was, for instance, Octave Feuillet. This was also doubtless owing in a measure to the fact that Augier's view of life, as shown in his plays, was abhorrent to such a cynic as was the great writer —trusted friend and confidant of the Empress Eugenie—Prosper Mérimée.

Émile Augier was proud of the fact that he was a grandson of the cheerfully licentious writer, Pigault-Lebrun, who had lived at La Celle Saint Cloud, a fact which had been impressed on me as a child. Pigault-Lebrun's life covered a remarkable span of French history, for he was born in 1753, in the reign of Louis the Fifteenth, and he lived till 1835, when Louis Philippe was king.

Augier died before real old age had touched him, which was strange when one remembers the easy happy life he had always led, and the fact that his mother, like her father, Pigault-Lebrun, lived till over eighty. . . .

But what mattered to me, at Croissy, was not the man regarded, then, as the modern Molière. Madame Déroulède, Jeanne, and Paul were what mattered, for they all three filled my heart then, and have remained there.

Jeanne, like myself, was far more mature than the girls with whom I spent so much of my time at La Celle Saint Cloud. Also she had a strong, exuberant sense of humour. I remember her as almost always laughing and chuckling, sometimes at a joke of her own, sometimes at a joke made against herself. She was far more alive and, to me, far more interesting, than pretty Lucie Guiard, daughter of Madame Déroulède's only sister, who also lived at Croissy, and who played the part in Jeanne's life a sister might have played.

I took a lively interest in them all, and I used to enjoy meeting the younger son, André Déroulède, and his lively, charming young wife. Jeanne once gave me a comic account of how their marriage had come about. André, a professional soldier, was quite unlike his brother; he was of medium height, quiet in manner, shy, and dark. After having been away from his own country for a long time, engaged in some colonial war, he came back, to his mother's distress, with a long black beard. He longed for a home of his own, so his aunt and certain family friends began to look out for the kind of girl they thought would suit him as wife. But he shrank from the way such marriages were then arranged. And at last, rather against his will, he consented to go to a ball where he would be present as a guest, and not as a young man in search of a wife.

To the surprise of his hostess, he there made friends with a girl who, though vivacious and intelligent, was regarded as plain, and who was extremely young. She was a granddaughter, which fact may have attracted André, of an esteemed Alsatian patriot called Dollfuss. They met again, and *pourparlers* were started.

But the girl said firmly that though she liked André Déroulède, and thought him "sympathetic," a word which in France spells almost everything, she could never bring herself to marry a man with a beard. This all but put a complete end to the affair, and that although André was aware that the then French Army chiefs only tolerated a bearded officer who was actually stationed in some part of France's colonial empire.

Jeanne, meanwhile, got in touch with the determined young woman. She liked her and, as she said to me, thought her so unlike André she was sure they would suit each other! So when she next saw her brother, she begged him earnestly to shave off his beard. He observer, "But supposing she doesn't like me clean-shaven? I shall have lost both my beard and my girl." Jeanne declared it was shocking of a soldier to show himself so cautious and lacking in courage, and she so worked on his feelings that one day he suddenly appeared at Croissy with only a moustache. His marriage took place six weeks later. I thought them an exceptionally happy couple, though, to the sorrow of Madame Déroulède, they remained childless.

I used to wonder what Jeanne did with herself all day, and then a chance visit made me acquainted with the fact that she accomplished a great deal of dull, slogging work for the *Ligue de Patriotes*. Paul entrusted her with answering what were often ignorant and stupid queries which arrived daily from every part of France. Apart from these letters written by his sister, nothing connected with Déroulède's public life impinged in any way on life as led in his mother's house.

My brother and I became members of the *Ligue des Patriotes*, and I took in the weekly paper *Le Drapeau*. Hilaire went to some of Paul's meetings, and my mother, Jeanne, and I spent an exciting afternoon at a monster gathering held, I think, on the Champs de Mars, which the Government were evidently afraid to proscribe. We drove there in a big old-fashioned landau, drawn by two aged horses which crawled through the masses of *liguers*, none of whom guessed that Jeanne was their President's sister.

Aunt Lily, when my mother wrote and told her of our expedition, expressed great relief that we had not run into serious danger of being pulled out of the carriage and held to ransom "by certain bad elements in the crowd"; so little did even a highly intelligent woman understand the working-people of her own beloved city. But Parisians of her generation remembered the Commune, and the fearful things which had happened during the final days of the rising which had followed the end of the Franco-Prussian War.

Déroulède made but one mistake during his arduous selfless work for France. But it was a most serious mistake, which delighted his enemies, and permanently injured his reputation in England. Fortunately it had curiously little effect on the way he was regarded by the working men and women of France. This serious mistake was his participation in what may be called the Boulangist affair.

It should surely be recognized, as it certainly is not, by every British writer when dealing with the Third French Republic, that what brought about the fall of France in June, 1940 was no new thing in French public life. There were a few "just men," but they were always in a minority. Laval is an eternal type, as old as human nature, and by no means confined to French human nature; but in the Third Republican régime, such men found the perfect soil in which to grow and expand into venal politicians. And, as was only too natural, his loathing and contempt for the French government of that day, made Déroulède eager to use any means which would bring about its downfall.

To those who were then interested in French politics—there were but few then so interested in England—it was easy to understand why General Boulanger attracted a certain type of honest patriotic Frenchman. The view, now apparently held by most historians, that he was an adventurer or, at least, a soldier of fortune, is a false view. The fact that Barthélemy Saint Hilaire was a friend of his father, and was chief witness at the future general's marriage disposes, I feel, of that story. On the other hand, Saint Hilaire told my aunt, in 1887, that he had always had a bad opinion of Boulanger.

I think few people are aware his mother was an Englishwoman. It was probably from her he acquired his fair hair, bright blue eyes, and remarkable good looks. In 1870, when his youth would have exempted him from active service, he insisted (as had done André Déroulède) on joining the Army, and he was severely wounded in one of the first battles of the campaign. He went back to his regiment before being passed fit; was again badly wounded, and again got back to the fighting line. When the war ended, Boulanger was one of the six youngest colonels in the French Army. At last, though backed by no political influence, he was made Minister for War, and he showed a determination and energy in carrying out certain long-needed reforms, especially with regard to the non-commissioned ranks, which were naturally approved and applauded by Déroulède. The two then came in touch for the first time. They had one quality in common. This was moral fearlessness. When the Orleans family was exiled, Boulanger wrote to the Duc d'Aumale an open letter, saying the Duc was at liberty to retain his rank of general in the French Army.

This is not the place to tell the story of Boulanger's hour of fame, and how he was at last backed with the vast fortune of the royalist Duchesse d'Uzès, who apparently believed he was ready to play the part of a General Monk. But before that happened, the President of the *Ligue des Patriotes*, obviously hoping to find in Boulanger a French Cromwell, helped him with all his might.

It is within my knowledge that Clemenceau warned Déroulède that Boulanger, though a fine soldier and an honest man, was quite incapapble of becoming what is called in France "a supreme chief." Yet there was a time when it looked as though the Third Republic was about to be destroyed. But fortunately for the more or less worthless group of men who then ruled France, Boulanger had been devoted for years to Madame de Bonnemains, a lady separated from her husband. She returned his love, and when she learnt he was in danger of being arrested and tried on a charge of high treason, she persuaded him to fly in disguise to Belgium. This was the end of everything for a man for whom hundreds of thousands of Frenchmen had been ready to risk their lives, and for whom many did risk, and lose, their reputations.

I happened to be spending a few days in Paris during the height of Boulanger's popularity, and I heard a good deal of the kind of political gossip which is never published. A man on terms of friendship at the Élysée told me the President of the Republic was terrified of what might be going to happen. As for the ministers, they were so alarmed that a secret price of a hundred thousand francs was put on the General's head. And, according to Paul Déroulède, who with characteristic generosity of nature said no word against the man who had betrayed his trust, it was the knowledge her lover was in peril of assassination which caused Madame de Bonnemains to act as she did.

As time went on, we were seldom at La Celle Saint Cloud, and so naturally only saw the Déroulèdes at long intervals. But how close and dear were the ties which had, and still, bound us, was shown by a letter written by Paul in the spring of 1891, within a few days of Madame Déroulède's death. He wrote:

"I was at Angoulême, having left my mother, perhaps more suffering than usual, but in much the same state as she had been for almost exactly twenty years. One evening I received a telegram from my sister saying our mother had a cold, but that I was not to feel anxious. However, I went home the next day, and to my relief found her only coughing a little, and with her eyes bright with joy at my unexpected return. She showed no surprise at seeing me, and she was not even surprised at my sitting up all the following night in her room. I did so now and again, for she slept badly, and I used sometimes to read to her for a couple of hours, so that the time might seem less long."

He then described the days that followed and how, though Madame Déroulède did not really seem much worse than usual, they felt vaguely anxious. At last the doctor suggested a specialist should see her; but all he said was he was amazed she had lived so long.

Paul's letter concluded with the words:

"Thank God she was never delirious, and her mind never wandered. When André, and his wife, Hélène, whom we had to send for in haste, arrived, she said a few words to them, and André kissed her hand. Then she shut her eyes, and did not open them again for six hours, when she ceased to breathe.

"Ah! my dear friend, it is not she who suffers now. It is we who suffer. I have never gone through such anguish as during the last few days. I feel as if my heart were torn in two. I did not know a human being could be as unhappy as I am feeling now. Every mother should be not only the source of life, but the source of joy, of happiness, of kindness, to her children. And such our mother was to us. I know that some day there will strike the hour of resignation, but she now fills all my thoughts and all my heart."

Déroulède had a peculiar hatred of those called by him internationalists. To his mind they were at the best misguided fools.

But he admitted there were very few of them. He longed for France and England to say together to Germany, "You are either against us or for us," and he never forgot the Kaiser had once spoken of holding France as a hostage.

In 1899, this valiant man made a vigorous attempt to destroy the Republican régime as then constituted. He was tried for high treason and, to the dismay of the French Government, was acquitted. The following year, in 1900, he received an arbitrary sentence of ten years' banishment.

He and Jeanne went to Saint Sebastian, just within the Spanish border, and settled there. His political enemies hoped that with its President in exile, the *Ligue des Patriotes* would dissolve. But to their surprise and chagrin, many new members were at once enrolled, and there was a great coming and going to Saint Sebastian.

Further, the feeling among many ordinary decent French men and women, whatever their political views, became suddenly exceedingly disturbed at the knowledge that such an honest patriot as, after all, they knew him to be, should be living in exile. To give but one example, in a preface written by the Imperialist, François Coppée, apropos of the banishment of Victor Hugo by the Government of Napoleon the Third, Coppée wrote:

"The Second Empire is not alone in bearing such a stain. We see to-day the spectacle of the poet, Paul Déroulède, exiled by the Republican Government in spite of the fine patriotic verses with which he consoled our country after the terrible reverses of 1870–71. The benevolence and nobility of his character is admitted by every true Frenchman. Yet Paul Déroulède is still at St. Sebastian, while Victor Hugo, three years after he was banished, was given permission to return to France. In this respect the Republic has nothing to cast at the Empire."

At last, Déroulède, after an exile which had lasted five full years, benefited by a political armistice, and to the surprise and horror of the then Government, the workers of Paris gave him a finer ovation than any Frenchman returning home had ever received, with the exception of that given to Napoleon after one of his great victories. It was estimated that a million Parisians turned out of their homes, and lined the streets to welcome him back.

During the few years which elapsed between his return to his country and the August of 1914, our dear friend went on doing his best to prepare France for the war he knew to be inevitable and, at a time when England was regarded with but tepid liking, he was a strong adherent of the *Entente Cordiale.*

His nature was without even a touch of the bitterness which is to be found in so many Frenchmen. But he never made the mistake of underestimating the country he regarded as France's deadly enemy. Not only had he taught himself German, he had a considerable knowledge of German literature.

After his return from exile, public opinion, as regarded his personality, had so changed that he would have been eagerly welcomed in many of the *salons* which then played a great rôle in Paris life. This was partly because there had grown up a feeling of shame and distress at the mean and infamous way in which he had been treated. But though he occasionally would accept an invitation to dinner, it was only from a hostess he knew to be in sympathy, overt or secret, with the views few men and women of his own world shared, even at that late hour.

Now and again, to his surprise, some writer who was highly thought of by his fellows, would come out into the open and praise him. Thus it gave him intense pleasure when Maurice Barrès wrote a splendid eulogy of his play on Du Guesclin. The play was not a success, for he had nothing of his uncle's gift for

-€ 65 }-

the theatre.

Paul Déroulède came to England twenty-nine years, almost to a day, after our first meeting. This was on the outbreak of the last war, and my brother, with whom he had kept in touch, brought him to see me. Though he was by then an old man, he seemed in my eyes scarcely changed, and his exceptionally tall figure was as upright as it had been when I was just seventeen and he thirty-nine.

He spoke with an almost painful joy and emotion of the fact that England and France were now fighting side by side, but he declared, what at the time very few believed, that the struggle would be long and hard.

My brother left us; we spoke of the distant past, of Jeanne's youth and mine; I shrank, however, from mentioning Madame Déroulède. But when I accompanied him to the door of my house, he took my hand and, holding it, he said, "When I think of my mother, your image often rises before me, for she loved you so truly, and I know that you, too, loved her."

It was an added grief to me, when almost everything in the dear familiar room where I had had the joy of seeing Paul Déroulède once more, was bombed and burnt in the May of 1941, to know that what his eyes had rested on that day, had vanished for ever. But the house where I spent over thirty happy years, and the door where I said goodbye to him, are still in being, and I look at them every time I leave my present home.

His death occurred in the autumn of 1914. I am happy in the thought he lived to know of the Battle of the Marne. And the other day I felt much moved when a well-known Frenchman, now in *La France Combattante*, told me that Clemenceau had asked Jeanne Déroulède to be present at Versailles when peace was signed in 1919. But I was not surprised to learn that she had not availed herself of the kindly meant invitation.

VI

As I look back on that summer, I feel as if I were again enveloped in what were to me such delightful currents of friendship and of kindness.

I had felt painfully apart from the life led round me in Sussex by the young people with whom I came in contact. From Jane Austen, onwards, this kind of life has been described in innumerable English novels. But not one of the writers, with the exception of Anthony Trollope, seems to have realized the part that money, even though in those days never mentioned, played in country house life. We were really poor, and so I could never join in the driving, the riding, and the coming and going to country houses, and occasionally to London, which filled the lives of my contemporaries. Also, though I was, even then, exceedingly interested in human nature, I felt out of sympathy with the kind of love-affairs, or perhaps I ought to say the near love-affairs, which played a considerable part in the imaginations of the girls with whom I was constantly thrown.

At La Celle Saint Cloud, there was not only no talk of love, the atmosphere was like that of the Heaven in which there is to be no marriage and giving in marriage. Every French girl among my new friends knew she would certainly marry in due course and, to use an expression that did not come into use for many a long year, "that was that."

No St. Cyr cadet, of the group who danced at the château each Sunday afternoon, singled out for special attention any of his partners. It is, however, fair to add that these young men were all under twenty, and no girl yet eighteen. Some of the girls were exceptionally attractive, and one of them was beautiful, as well as lively and amusing. She was the younger sister of Odette de la Pommeraye, who had been engaged, almost from childhood, to one of the St. Cyr cadets, whom she married in due time.

In our neighbourhood there was only one man of marriageable age. His name was George Fontenel; he was a barrister; and he spent every summer with his parents, who lived on the way to Rueil. As he played a certain part in my life, and his personality has remained very present in my mind for nearly sixty years, I propose to describe him and his family.

As they lived some way from La Celle Saint Cloud, they were not among our Curé's parishioners, so I did not meet them every Sunday, and on all the other occasions when we went to church, as I did all our neighbours. But the Fontenels had been long acquainted with my grandmother, and my mother and my aunts regarded them as family friends.

Monsieur and Madame Fontenel both belonged to what was then called in France *la haute bourgeoisie* and, alone among our acquaintances, they approximated to what is still the English view of people of their class in France. Madame Fontenel had no knowledge of, and no interest in, any country but her own. She was exceedingly narrow-minded, and though truly religious, she had but little sympathy with her kind. Physically she was tall and thin. She looked under-vitalized, and her manner was cold and distant. She still wore mourning for a child she had lost nearer thirty than twenty years before, and her whole life was centred round her son and daughter, especially her son.

Monsieur Fontenel was a small stout man, very kindly and good-humoured in nature and in manner. But to one accustomed to the forthright simplicity and straightforwardness of the older men of my own family, he appeared extremely affected. He never met us without kissing my hand, as well as that of my mother, and he had an odd way of throwing his eyes up to heaven when he wished to emphasize some point he was making. I cannot remember what were his political opinions, but there can be no doubt he held, in a probably intensified form, the dislike and contempt for the Third Republic which seemed endemic among almost all the educated French people of his day.

During many years of my life I strongly believed people have the children they deserve; as also that certain family traits are always transmitted from members of one generation to another. With time, both these theories have become much modified. I still hold that it is rare for a boy or girl to "go wrong" if he or she had the good fortune to possess kind, unselfish, loving parents. I know, however, how mistaken I then was in my view that men and women almost always inherit their parents' characters and peculiarities.

Riette and George Fontenel was extraordinarily unlike their father and mother. Riette, at the time of which I write, must have been twenty-seven, that is ten years older than I, which even now appears, and indeed is, in many ways, a much greater difference when a girl is seventeen than is the case in later life. She had a mature and, as I now realize, a cynical view of life. Also, in addition to being extremely intelligent, she was blessed with what her parents completely lacked—a strong and puckish sense of fun. She wrote and spoke English well, and was familiar with the English literature of that day. Madame Fontenel must have been an elegant, even a good-looking woman in youth. But Riette was extremely plain—what in America is called homely—and she made not the smallest effort to "make the best of herself." It was supposed, in our neighbourhood, she had decided to remain unmarried, as now and again, though extremely seldom, happened with a certain type of young Frenchwoman.

My mother was fond of Riette Fontenel, owing to the following circumstance. When aged about eighteen, Riette had met the then well-known writer, my mother's closest friend, Mrs. Rundle Charles, on a visit to our house, and she had become enthralled both by that lady's singularly charming personality, and also by her novels, especially *The Chronicles of the Schönberg-Cotta Family,* still, then, a famous book. This shows Riette Fontenel to have been exceptionally broad-minded, for she was a devout Catholic, and Martin Luther is the central figure and hero of that historical novel. One day, when alone with my mother and Mrs. Charles, she confided to them her intention of remaining single unless she could find a man who genuinely attracted her, and whom she genuinely attracted. She added she would also only marry a person who, like herself, was a practising Catholic. She had evidently not met any man who fulfilled these two conditions, by the time I first became, in a real sense, acquainted with her.

George Fontenel seemed to have nothing in common with his parents and sister, and of him I have retained a kind, and even a tender, feeling. He had not acquired Riette's knowledge of foreign languages, and while quite as well read and as cultivated as were my cousins, he appeared to have none of the cheerful, eager outlook on life they shared with one another, different as they happened to be. He was tall and slight, and I now see that physically he was very like his mother. But as he had a frank, kind, and simple manner, this fact then escaped my notice.

On the first Sunday after our arrival at La Celle Saint Cloud, while we were on our way to a stretch of wild woodland which in my childhood had been called *Chez l'Empereur,* for it was the private property of Napoleon the Third, we met the father and son. While Monsieur Fontenel was overwhelming my mother with flowery compliments, and expressions of delight that she had come back to spend the summer in the neighbourhood, George and I stood apart. We made friends, and I liked his easy, unaffected approach. He and his father accompanied us on our way, and I discovered George and I had certain literary tastes in common.

The same evening there arrived a stiff note from Madame Fontenel, asking us to *goûter* the following afternoon.

My mother was expecting a friend from Paris, so she suggested I, alone, should accept the invitation; and not from any conventional feeling, but because there happened to be a long and rather lonely stretch of road between La Celle Saint Cloud and the Fontenel property, she said Nurse had better accompany me. To that I vigorously objected, and she gave way.

However, the moment I arrived at the Fontenels' house, I realized my hostess could hardly believe it possible I had been allowed to walk there unattended by a maid and, in spite of her exaggerated civility of manner, she could not conceal the horror she felt at such a thing having happened. As for Riette, she burst into harsh laughter, evidently equally amused by my discomfiture and Madame Fontenel's dismay.

While the three of us were having *goûter* in the pleasantly cool dining-room of their pretty old house, the mother and daughter put me through a careful examination, obviously intended to discover how I had been educated, what sort of life I led in England, and, finally, whether I cared for France and French life. They were both pleased to hear I had been in a convent school for two years. But Riette was evidently shocked and puzzled as she gradually discovered how ill-educated I had been, if indeed I had been educated at all, from her point of view. She recalled my mother's good knowledge of German, and thought it strange indeed I had not been taught that language.

After a while an old woman came in. She had been, I was told, Riette's and George's nurse. She was asked to sit down and share our very delicious *goûter*, and my heart warmed to Madame Fontenel, when I saw how kind she was in manner to the dour-looking old nurse. All the same, I felt sure she had been only told to sit down, and join in the meal, so as to have a good look at me. The opinion of devoted family servants was highly valued in those days by French people of a certain class. There are frequent, and always kindly, references to their maids in many of my grandmother's and aunts' letters.

After Riette and George's one-time nurse had left the dining-room, I was suddenly asked whether I intended to follow in the Belloc tradition and become an artist. Even Riette was evidently surprised that both my aunts, though married women with children, had kept up their painting, and often exhibited. I replied that though my mother would have liked me to become an artist, I wished to be a writer. My inquisitors approved, on the whole, of this intention, and Madame Fontenel said something implying she supposed I would write children's books, as had done Madame Swanton Belloc. But Riette was shrewd enough to know that this was not likely to be my ideal; she threw me a funny look, and observed she felt sure I intended to write novels. As to that she was right, though many years were to go by before I wrote my first novel.

At last, to my relief, the father and son joined us, and I noticed Monsieur Fontenel throwing an anxious and questioning look at his wife. This did not surprise me, for I already suspected they were wondering if I might prove a desirable daughter-in-law. Before my father's death, it had become known in the neighbourhood that my mother had been left a considerable sum of money by an uncle, so it was reasonable for the Fontenels to assume I should be given a dowry on my marriage, and, on my mother's death, inherit half her fortune. But that this would affect the views of George's parents, did not then occur to me.

At last I thought it was time I went home, and Monsieur Fontenel at once said he and his son would accompany me and my maid to La Celle Saint Cloud. I can still see the look of rather malicious amusement on Riette's face when she explained that I had walked from there by myself. However, both George and

Monsieur Fontenel were far too well bred to show any surprise at this astonishing bit of information.

Within a day or two, George, accompanied by his sister, called at our house; and at once Riette and my mother became as they had been about ten years before, on affectionate terms. Riette borrowed one of our English library books, and it was soon brought back by George, who told me he had just bought a camera, and would like to come and take my photograph and that of the house. It was settled he and Riette should come on an afternoon I had already arranged to invite some of my friends. So within a few days, after what was supposed to be an English tea, prepared with considerable trouble by myself and Nurse, we all went out to the *pré*, a meadow just beyond our garden, which consisted of a field and a little wood. I loved our *pré*, and had often longingly gone back to it in thought, during the years I had lived in England.

I lately found a copy of the photograph George Fontenel took of me that afternoon, and it gives a clear picture of what I was like at that time of my life. I am in a white dress, and wearing a large straw hat. George asked me to tip the hat back so as to show my face. That face is very young and serious-looking, and my hair, of which I had an immense amount, is parted in the middle, at a time when every woman under fifty, and often over fifty, had a fringe.

A week later George and I happened, by a most unusual chance, to be alone for a few moments, and I asked him what photographs he had taken since we had last met. He answered he had not photographed anything since then, and he went on to explain, speaking in a quiet, matter-of-fact way, that he had only bought the camera in order to possess a portrait of me. That was the only occasion when he ever said a word implying that he had any feeling for me apart from that of ordinary liking. But I had very soon realized he was falling in love with me, and I felt amused, pleased, and thrilled. I kept what I thought I had come to know, to my-self, and I believed my mother to be quite unaware of what was becoming increasingly clear to me. But after a while, something occurred which showed that as to this I was wrong.

Early one afternoon, the bell which was outside our gate rang and, as was nearly always the case when that happened, for Nurse was already old by then, and slow-moving, I ran out to see who was there. It was Monsieur Fontenel and George, who had come to ask me to accompany them on a walk through the woods which were by far the most delightful feature of the neighbour-hood. So I hurried indoors to tell my mother I should be out for over an hour. But to my great surprise and vexation she said I must go and explain I could not leave the house, as she wanted me to do something with her. I was disappointed, and also puz-zled, for she looked sad, and what she very seldom looked, stern, as well.

And then, when I went back into the *grand salon,* she aston-ished me by saying she felt sure my father would not have ap-proved of my taking a walk with Monsieur Fontenel and his son. This was the first time she had ever spoken of my father in con-nection with my conduct, and I felt bewildered and distressed. But very soon, with her usual directness and honesty, she went on to say she had noticed with unease and fear the increasingly fre-quent visits of George Fontenel to our house, as she felt certain his family would not wish him to marry a girl who had had so unconventional an upbringing, who was half English, and who would have no dowry.

She observed it would be painful, as well as unpleasant, should I become a source of contention between George and his devoted parents.

I saw it was costing her a great deal to say all this to me, and I know, now, she must have been telling herself that, but for the loss of the money she had inherited—a loss owing to what she had come to believe had been her own culpable folly—I might have made what from the point of view of my French family, would have been an ideal marriage.

I soon knew she had been right for, as the days of that summer and autumn drifted by, it became obvious George's mother and sister had begun to regard his liking for me with fear and distaste. They must also have soon discovered we had very little money, and probably concluded the old story of my mother's large legacy to have been idle gossip.

Yet, so strange is human nature, George's parents evidently became annoyed when they discovered how constantly we dined at Croissy. Monsieur Fontenel even called one day, having, I suppose, first ascertained I was out and, for once putting aside his affected, sugary manner, said he thought he ought to tell my mother how ill people thought of Paul Déroulède, and of how absurd and dangerous was Déroulède's insane belief in a future war between France and Germany. He told her of a tour he and Riette had made in Germany two years before, and how struck they had been by the courtesy and kindness with which they had been treated. He further said—which offended my mother—he felt sure the Germans disliked the English very much more than they disliked the French. Long afterwards she told me she had formed the impression Monsieur Fontenel had come prepared to say something concerning George's liking for me. There was a strong affection between father and son, and Monsieur Fontenel must naturally have longed to see George happily settled in life. But no doubt annoyed at my mother's refusal to accept his view either of Paul Déroulède's activities, or of the German dislike for England, the old gentleman, as I always thought of him as being, had thought better of saying even a cautious word to one he certainly regarded as an obstinate and eccentric Englishwoman.

Before we went back to England, the brother and sister, accompanied by their father, came to bid us good-bye, and my mother told them she hoped to come back the following summer, as our stay at La Celle Saint Cloud had given such pleasure to me and to my brother.

Knowing all I now know of French life, I am inclined to think that Madame Fontenel, up to the day we left La Celle Saint Cloud that autumn, thought it possible some kind of approach to George's parents might be made through my aunt, Madame Ballot. This would have placed them in a delicate position, for their son was thirty, indifferent to money, and earning an income at the Bar. Also, he was obviously a man who knew his own mind, though so far he had not told them what his mind was.

My aunt did not know then, and was never told later, of our having seen a good deal of the Fontenels that summer. As for me, in a sense so far older than my years, and with the peculiar views of life partly induced by my French blood, my intimacy with Aunt Lily, and my hearty contempt at the undercurrent of talk concerning the delights of falling in love which I had heard during my life in Sussex, I thought over the matter as though I were outside it.

I had become fond of George Fontenel, and I thought very well of him; but I did not care for either of his parents, and his sister I actually disliked. I was not, as were most of the English girls I knew, in love with love. I longed to be a writer, and to become part of the literary world, which I then supposed to be a paradise. Also, though I had no warrant for such a belief, I fully expected to be married some day. Well do I recall the satiric amusement aroused when, on being asked by some inquisitive persons in Slindon if I was engaged, I innocently answered, "Not yet." So, though it made me sad to leave France, that sadness was not intensified by the fact that I had left as good and faithful a friend as I believed George Fontenel would always be.

Early in the New Year, my mother handed me a marriage *faire-part,* which had the honour of informing the reader of the forth-coming nuptials of Mademoiselle Henriette Fontenel and Monsieur Henri Fortoul. I wondered if this *faire-part* was the precursor of one which would announce the marriage of George and of some girl chosen by his mother. But I did not think this likely, for I knew he had a strong will of his own, though I doubted if either of his parents was aware of it.

We spent eight weeks at La Celle Saint Cloud in the depth of the following winter, I suppose because our Sussex house was again let, and we had nowhere else to go. My mother had passed the first winter of her married life in our French home, and as she now lived mentally much in the past, she did not feel, as I did, the loneliness and the bitter cold. The oil froze in our lamps, as did the ink in the inkstands—indeed those weeks contained the only days when I felt life scarcely endurable. We occasionally went into Paris but, when there, we naturally saw nothing of the Fontenel family.

And now for the end of an episode which may seem too slight to have been worth the telling.

One day, I think in the following April, my mother, who I knew had received a long letter from Aunt Lily, said she feared I was going to have a painful shock, as she had bad news from Paris. My heart at once flew to my cousins and, in this showing myself a true Frenchwoman, I wondered, with a sharp pang, whether any of Juliette's children had died.

Mamma gave me the last pages of Aunt Lily's letter, and told me to read it after she had gone out. She had a great shrinking from giving pain, and though we each loved each other so dearly, no parent and child with so many interests and tastes in common, could ever have been more unlike than were my mother and myself. She never knew what was going on in my heart, or even in my mind.

To return to the pages of the letter she left, that spring, in my hand. It ran:

"I know you will be grieved to learn the dreadful misfortune which has befallen our old friends and neighbours, Monsieur and Madame Fontenel. They have lost their only son.

"He was riding in the Bois, on a hired horse of whose peculiarities he was unaware, when the horse bolted, and flung him against a tree. His right leg was badly bruised, but he thought the injury of no importance, as he was able to walk after it had occurred. But the bruise inflamed, and he was laid up for some time. Becoming weary of inaction, and hearing of a physician who claims to cure people with some form of rubbing, he sent for him. The physician rubbed the place which had been bruised, and blood poisoning developed. The rest was only a matter of days.

"You know enough of these poor people to know they are sincerely religious, and the unfortunate young man met death with courage and resignation, his one thought being to soothe his parents' terrible grief."

Riette, in answer to our letters of condolence, wrote my mother a horrible account of the way her brother had been mismanaged by the doctor she believed had caused his death.

That summer I was allowed to go to La Celle Saint Cloud for a short time, accompanied by a woman who was an admixture of useful maid and chaperon. We lived in the chalet and, excepting when I dined with the Sirys, or lunched out, I never had enough to eat, for the lady had never learned any cooking. Although I can cook, I hate the sight of raw meat and raw fish, so when at home I lived on eggs.

I had been at the chalet for some days, when Juliette asked

me, one evening, whether I intended to call on the Fontenels. I replied that I did not like to do so, as George and his father had so often come to our house, I thought it would sadden them to see me. To that she made no comment; and then took place a meeting which has remained as present to me as though it had just happened.

I was walking back, by myself, from seeing an English friend to the tramway passing by La Jonchère to Rueil, when I saw Monsieur and Madame Fontenel, with Riette, and a stranger I at once knew must be her husband, standing outside their gate. I was still some way from the gate, and in two minds as to what to do. Had it been possible, I would have turned round and waited till they had gone into their garden. But I believed they had almost certainly seen me, so I walked on.

When I was close to the gate, Monsieur Fontenel suddenly detached himself from the others and, rushing forward, folded me in his arms. He burst out crying, and I could not help crying too. Madame Fontenel gave a stifled moan, and Riette, her eyes streaming with tears, and followed by her husband, hurried her mother through the gate. By then, Monsieur Fontenel had drawn my arm through his, constantly pressing me convulsively closer and closer to him. Then he began walking with me up the road towards La Celle Saint Cloud.

At last he told me that, just after George's death, the old nurse had shown them, pinned inside a curtain which hung round his bed, a copy of the photograph he had taken of me in our field. George had asked her to place the photograph so that when he was dying he could see it, without any of those about him being aware it was there.

The poor father kept exclaiming, "He loved you! He loved you!" and in between these heart-rending cries he spent the rest of the time, till we reached the chalet, telling me every painful detail connected with his son's illness.

The days and nights that followed were filled, for me, with pain and acute distress. I had never come in real contact with death—death, to me still the most inexplicable of all mysteries. I also valued, even then more than is usual, that rarest of all human attributes, selfless affection. And I knew I had lost that kind of affection in losing this friend. It was in vain I reminded myself, while I lay sobbing during those summer nights, how slight had been our acquaintance, for I felt something precious had gone out of my life, something I might never find again.

There are four lines I feel might have been written for George Fontenel and the girl for whom he cared:

> "Ne pleure pas, toi que j'amais.
> Ce qui n'est plus ne fut jamais."
> "Laisse couler ma douleur sombre,
> Une ombre peut pleurer une ombre."

Many years later I had an intimate friend who was a spiritualist. She was surrounded by those who shared her beliefs, and one day she said to me, "A medium to whom I went yesterday has received a message for you from a man with a queer name." And she produced a piece of paper on which was written *Fontenel*. Had I not been a Catholic, I would have gone to her medium and tried to get in touch with George. But Catholics are not allowed to practise any form of spiritualism.

VII

FOND as I had now become of certain of my French relations of whom I had only retained somewhat vague memories, the one of them all I really loved, and who had a considerable influence on my life as a young woman, was my aunt, Lily Ballot. She was two years older than my father; they were closely united during his forty-two years of life; and she had shown me and my brother, from our birth, the deepest affection.

She once told my mother, who became after her marriage Lily's one beloved and trusted woman friend, that she had had a delightful childhood, never scolded by the mother with whom she had an unusually tender tie, and adored by the father whose favourite sitter she became from the age of two, till he gave up painting. She was never bored when sitting to him as a little child, for he spent the time telling her exciting and amusing fairy tales of which the scene was laid in the woods where each spring, summer, and autumn she and her brother gathered flowers and mushrooms.

My younger aunt was of medium height, and remained slender and graceful far beyond middle age. Her fair hair was naturally wavy; she had dark-blue eyes; and her features retained their delicate perfection to the end of her life. Surprisingly unlike, both in appearance and in character, her mother and her sister, each also so different from the other, she was said to be physically like her father's eldest sister, Mélanie Belloc, Baronne Le Roy, who lived, in full possession of all her wits, to the age of eighty-eight.

My beloved aunt must have had, till bitter loss and sorrow touched her, a joyous, high-spirited nature, and even as a child she wrote letters filled with an unusual quality of life. Thus to Adelaide de Montgolfier there came, one winter day, when the writer was only ten years old:

"My dear godmother, I will not do what you ask, for I think it unreasonable to require a child to do what you want me to do. I owe obedience to my mother, and should she require me to do what I consider unreasonable, I shall do it. But Maman is never unreasonable."

Lily and her sister, Louise, were only united as to one thing —this was in their determination to prevent Mademoiselle de Montgolfier from playing any part in their lives. When Lily was sixteen, one of her Chasseriau cousins fell so much in love with her that his condition, as described in a letter written by Lily's mother to her own sister, Madame de Gon, was *pitoyable*. The Hilaire Bellocs had never been able to save money, and the only dowry either daughter was to receive on her marriage was ten thousand francs (four hundred pounds). This money had been left to them by their uncle, Armand Swanton. He had become very fond of them when they were children, and he determined to save each year for his two nieces something from what was, and is, the meagre pay of a French officer. Thus the twenty thousand francs must have represented much self-denial on his part; and both Lily and Louise lived to feel extremely grateful to him. Even so, to Mademoiselle, this minute dowry was as she frankly stated, *dérisoire*. So she was horrified when Lily Belloc said firmly that nothing would induce her to become Baronne Frédéric Chasseriau, and that however truly her cousin loved her, and however long he was willing to wait in the hope she would change her mind. How wise was this decision was proved

two years later when she made a most happy marriage to a young
barrister named Philippe Millet. They had two children, and
then, when his son was six, and his daughter two years old,
Philippe died of typhoid, a disease which for over a hundred years
has been the scourge of France. Within a few months Lily also
lost her little girl, to be mourned by her silently as long as her
life endured.

Aunt Lily must have been forty-five when I first remember
her. She was still beautiful and, what counts for so much more
than beauty to my thinking, dowered with enchanting gifts of
sympathy and kindness. Though compelled to be always careful
about money, she was also understandingly generous. She used
to come to La Celle Saint Cloud about once a week, and it must
have been a long tiring journey to a woman who had never been
strong. But she brought joy, as well as almost always welcome
gifts, to the fatherless little Marie and Hilaire. Her mother and
the English sister-in-law, with both of whom she had so curiously
little in common—her one pleasure was painting, as her godmother had early wearied her of literature and of foreign languages—leaned on her, asked her advice, and, above all, loved her.
How I regret, now, never having questioned her concerning oh!
so many things I long to know concerning my own and my
brother's forebears. But in those days, and for long afterwards, I
thought those dear to me would live for ever, and my mind was
centred in the present.

By the time of my parents' marriage in the early autumn of
1877, Lily had married again, and was the wife of a barrister
named Charles Ballot. Their only child, named Marcel, was seven.

All through my childhood the only person of whom I felt
afraid was Uncle Charles. He was tall and dark; his mother had
been partly Spanish, and he was unlike any man who ever came
to our house. Yet, though I was then naturally unaware of it,

he belonged to a not uncommon type of Frenchman: the austere, one-track-minded, highly honourable type, who willingly dies for his convictions, and who, partly because he never leaves his own country, knows nothing, and has no wish to know anything, of the world outside France. This type of educated Frenchman is almost always unknown even in the England which believes itself intimately acquainted with France.

Charles Ballot had a cold, and what I felt to be a forbidding, manner. Yet my mother had a genuine affection for him, as well as a great respect, and it used to puzzle her that his wife would so often disagree with him concerning matters he had much at heart. All the same, even I, as an unobservant child, was well aware how devoted was my formidable Uncle Charles to my delightful Aunt Lily. His stern face would alter and light up when she threw him a challenging, teasing smile, and that even when she said something with which he was in total disagreement. But, most unfortunately for her, his was a jealous love. He was jealous not only of every man who came near her, but of her affection for her mother, her sister-in-law, and of the younger members of our family. "He would like to live with me on a desert island, without even a Man Friday!" she once exclaimed with unusual petulance. And, in a sense, that exclamation embodied the exact truth.

Born with the frank, expansive nature characteristic of every member of her father's family, Lily Ballot learned the difficult lesson of never telling her husband when she had seen, by appointment or by chance, some person—man or woman—she cherished in memory of what had been so happy and so free a youth, till her twenty-sixth year had brought her fearful loss, and an agonizing double sorrow.

Just after his death, she wrote and told my mother that on a certain day in the early 'eighties, she received one morning, while still in bed, a little box sent by hand. On opening it, she found there a gold bracelet, and at first she could not believe it was meant for her. Then she saw that inside the bracelet, in very small characters, were engraved the words "Silver wedding day," with two dates, "1858–1883." And in the same letter in which she told of this gift, she went on:

"I lay back on my pillow, and burst into tears, remembering how ungrateful I had shown myself during those twenty-five years of devoted, protecting love, and of what I now knew was unbounded kindness. How noble was Charles' whole existence— an existence comprised of fidelity, of hard work, and of tenderness! Yet because he was so unlike the men among whom I had been brought up, because he was so grave and reserved, and so little given to praise, I never gave him back love for love, as I should have done."

When I attained the age of what reason God meant me to possess, I used sometimes to wonder how Aunt Lily's marriage had come about. I knew all about her *mariage d'amour* to Philippe Millet, and I was even aware that, during her widowhood, a cousin of Mademoiselle de Montgolfier had wished to marry her. So I was astonished she had become the wife of a man who was, in every way, so unlike herself, and in whose presence my brother and I always felt uncomfortable. And then, one day, my mother told me what I think was a romantic story, and it altered my whole mental attitude to Uncle Charles.

On her husband's death Lily Millet, having become very poor, felt compelled to accept her parents' invitation to spend the winter of each year with them in their Paris *appartement*. To be once more a daughter at home was an unnatural existence, for a young woman who had enjoyed seven years of an unusually happy married life. Her brother, who had just had a terrible illness, was an invalid; and she daily had to endure the presence of her godmother, who spent almost every morning at 5 rue de l'Ecole de Médecine. Lily was not interested in the educational standards of the then children of France. She even deplored the efforts made to improve those standards made by her mother under, as she believed, the influence of Adelaide de Montgolfier. I recall feeling secretly much pleased when I once overheard my aunt exclaim, when my lack of understanding of the *Grammaire Française* was being deplored, "I am glad our Marie is not being turned into the Lilliputian learned monster of the kind Mademoiselle longed for me to be!"

The only thing which reconciled the young widow to what to her was so dreary a life each winter, was the joy her presence gave her father. But she only felt a measure of content during the summer months spent with her little son in the small house, set in a chestnut grove high up behind the church of La Celle Saint Cloud, where she had dwelt with Philippe Millet for seven years which had been filled with intense happiness and boundless love.

During those years there had been among her husband's friends a fellow barrister named Charles Ballot. He was a quiet, dour young man, very different in every way from the carefree, exuberant Philippe Millet. Yet the two had become intimate, and when Philippe fell seriously ill, Lily became aware that of all her husband's friends, it was Charles Ballot who showed himself genuinely disturbed and anxious. When came the awful blow of Philippe's death, she knew that even if he said little, Charles Ballot's sorrow was deeper than that of any one else in their circle. She once told my mother he had been the only man, apart from her father and brother, she had felt she could endure to see present at her husband's funeral.

During the first winter spent by her in the Paris home of her girlhood, Monsieur Ballot called on her from time to time, and showed a measure of affection for his dead friend's little boy. Then, to the surprise of both her parents and herself, fifteen months after Philippe's death, he called on her father, and said his one wish in life was to marry Hilaire Belloc's widowed daughter. Lily's answer was unequivocal. She refused to see him, and asked her father to write and say she had decided never to marry again. Charles Ballot accepted her decision, and no longer came to see her and her child.

As time went on, Lily Millet became anxious to earn a little money; and as she had been a favourite pupil of the then fashionable portrait painter, Charles Chaplin, she obtained a certain number of commissions. But she soon found that the only way for her to make even a very small regular income, would be by giving drawing lessons. Among her pupils was a young American lady who lived on the right bank of the Seine, and who was willing to pay a double fee if she could be given drawing lessons after dinner. So Lily arranged to spend two hours with this lady on three evenings of each week. Thus every Monday, Wednesday, and Friday, young Madame Millet walked through the ill-lit streets of the Paris of the 'fifties, from the heart of the *Quartier Latin* to the Place Vendôme.

She soon became aware that a man always followed her, from where she turned the corner of the quiet Cour du Commerce, out of which opened the even quieter rue de l'Ecole de Médecine, till she was within a few yards of the hotel where lived her American pupil. This occurred not only while she was on her way to give each of these drawing lessons, but while she was walking home as well. But the man always kept his distance, excepting when she was actually crossing the Seine. Then he would come close behind her, falling back as soon as she reached the quay. Though Lily was not aware of it, the Paris bridges were supposed to be unsafe after nightfall, for now and again walkers were set upon, everything in the way of money and, if a woman, jewels, being taken from them. Should the victim put up a fight, he or she ran the risk of being tossed over into the river.

Lily did not tell her parents she was being followed in this persistent way, for she was aware it would have caused them great alarm, the more so that, though she was now nearly thirty, they both treated her as if she was still a young girl. So she put up with what was, after all, an invisible presence. She came to believe, and even to hope, that the man who thus dogged her footsteps three times a week was a harmless, lonely God's fool who found a measure of comfort in his peculiar behaviour.

At last, when on her way home on a bitterly cold winter evening, she met with the kind of adventure she had not known she had to dread. She was half-way across the bridge when two footpads loomed up before her and roughly asked her to give them not only whatever money she had on her, but any bracelets and rings she might be wearing. Before she could make up her mind what to say or what to do, both her assailants had been struck down, and lay sprawling on the ground, while over them stood a man with a pistol in his hand. She heard a voice which seemed vaguely familiar call out, "Stop where you are—or I'll shoot . . ." He then blew a whistle, and two police agents ran forward from their station at the end of the bridge.

Lily's rescuer, without speaking, offered her his arm, and after they had reached the Quai Voltaire, she stopped and told him she could now make her way home alone. He still remained silent, and she said she hoped he would find time to call at 5 rue de l'Ecole de Médecine, so that her parents could give themselves the pleasure of thanking him for what he had done.

And then, at last, he spoke to her, and years after his death she repeated in a letter to my mother the words the man she had then supposed to be a stranger had uttered. They were: "You know me, Madame chérie, and I fear you cannot wish me to come and see your parents."

Charles Ballot, in his fear for her safety, had given up three evenings of each week to follow and protect her from the kind

of adventure which had just befallen her. She was so moved
by this proof of faithful love that just before they reached the
Cour du Commerce, she told him that if he was still of the same
mind as he had been four years before, she was willing to marry
him. During the twenty-seven years that followed she made
Charles Ballot a good, unselfish, and, what must have been far
more difficult to such a woman, an obedient, wife.

The fact that he went on adoring her as he did, was a source
of wonderment not only to herself, but to all those about her who
could only see in him a singularly reserved and unemotional man.
Yet by the time I was able to notice what was going on about me,
no one, however unperceptive, could have doubted his passionate
love for his wife, and his absorption in the only child with which
they were blessed after they had been married three years.

From the day Marcel Ballot was born, his father became exceedingly anxious to leave a little money to his son. So even at a
time when he was earning only moderate fees, till many years
later, when he received, as President of the Council of State under
the Third Republic, what was for France the considerable salary
of thirty thousand francs, he and my aunt always saved, at first
some hundreds, and later some thousands, of francs from their
yearly income. This was why they lived on the fifth floor of an
old house in the rue Volney, close to the Boulevard des Capucines.
Their *appartement* was, however, spacious, and my aunt's square
sitting-room was not over-filled with furniture, as was then the
fashion. There were a few comfortable armchairs, a deep sofa,
and a round First Empire table believed to have been in the
music-room at Malmaison, in the days of the Empress Josephine.
On the turquoise-blue walls hung a few good pictures.

But though they lived very simply, Aunt Lily and Uncle
Charles entertained more than did most of their friends after the
Franco-Prussian War; and I remember a luncheon party given
in honour of the then extremely young Austen Chamberlain.

He had been in Germany and, to the annoyance of his host and hostess, he talked with marked enthusiasm of Bismarck. Who then would have believed that this Englishman would live to become the noted statesman whose love for France was looked at askance by some of his fellows?

My cousin Marcel was quite unlike any member of his mother's family, and in no way recalled his father. He was extremely delicate, and, while he was still a pretty little boy, his mother wrote of him, "He is like one of those small works of art made in the eighteenth century; exquisitely fashioned, and as fragile as such a work of art is apt to be." But though his face had an expression of keen intelligence, as he grew into manhood he became very plain, and he was always unnaturally pale.

All through my childhood and early girlhood I was aware of the immense part he played in his parents' lives. So I knew how true a mark of their affection for my mother and for me it must have been, when they invited us to accompany them to the meeting of the French Academy where he was to be awarded the *Prix de Poésie* for an *Eloge de Lamartine*. We walked the whole way to the famous Coupole, Marcel between his parents, with Mamma and I just behind them. He was then twenty, and I just twelve years old.

This cousin of mine, to whom I became fondly attached, was in some ways the most singular human being I have ever known, and he certainly had the most original mind of any of Madame Swanton Belloc's grandchildren. Self-willed, and with a cynical outlook on life, he had no liking for the Republican régime to which his father had devoted his life. Also, what delighted and attracted me was something Uncle Charles entirely lacked, an all-round, agreeable sense of humour. As a quite young man his brilliant talk and mordant wit seemed inexhaustible, and these two attributes naturally made him eagerly welcomed in every kind of society. Thus he was as unlike his father as two men, belonging to the same race, and having received the same education, could well be.

From his mother he had inherited an unusual kindness of heart of which he was somewhat ashamed. A devoted and most kind son to both his parents, he never showed the irritation he must have constantly felt as a result of his mother's nervous fears concerning his health; and while listening silently to the frequent expression of his father's narrow, dogmatic, views of life.

Marcel was the only man among my relations who went through certain religious phases. He felt an intellectual interest in religion, and from when he grew up he became and remained what may be called a reluctant believer. His father and half-brother, René Millet, were what were then called agnostics, though their wives were convinced Christians. Aunt Lily's Catholicism was generous-hearted, and compassionate to all. Louise Millet was an unconscious Jansenist, of the *"De part la loi, défense à Dieu, de faire miracle en ce lieu"* type. The Redelspergers, father and son, were nominally Protestant. Étienne Siry ultimately returned to the Faith, perhaps influenced by a noble prayer written by his elder son, and found among the younger Siry's papers, after he had been killed at Bois des Fosses, on the sixth of February, 1918. My dear cousin, Juliette Siry, has always been a practising Catholic, as are her three daughters. One of her granddaughters, whose father was killed in the autumn of 1914 when she was three years old, is a nun. Charles du Bos, the husband of Juliette and Étienne Siry's youngest daughter, became a champion of the Church, as those familiar with his writings are aware.

To please his father, Marcel went to the Bar, and for a while practised in the Paris law courts. He even accepted the dull post of Secretary to the Lawyers' Association. But, in that proving himself a true chip of the Belloc block, he early decided to become a writer. His literary taste was fine and sure; and great was his pleasure when he was made dramatic critic of the *Figaro;* and even greater when, later, he became a Reader to the Théâtre Français. Alone of us all, he was early absorbed in the theatre, and in the art of the drama. When he was over thirty, in collaboration with Ambroise Janvier, he wrote a comedy called *Les Amants Légitimes.*

When the French Divorce Law had been drawn up in 1880, it had been hedged round with all sorts of restrictions, of which the most absurd ordained that if a divorced couple were ever discovered to be again on affectionate terms, the lady's dowry must be returned to her parents. Out of what had at once become a dead letter, Marcel and his friend wrote a most amusing play. It was perfectly cast, and it ran for a long time in Paris, being later constantly revived in the provinces.

This one success brought Marcel Ballot a good deal of money, but apart from what were his royalties from that play, he remained a poor man until, at the age of fifty, he was appointed *Agent Général* for the *Société des Auteurs Dramatiques,* which carries one of the few high salaries paid in France. The work involved was onerous, for it meant being in touch with not only every French playwright, but also with all those foreigners who wished to adapt French plays. The last time I saw him, not long before he died in 1928, was in the fine historic house, built in 1740, where the *Société* has its headquarters.

As I look back I realize how wonderfully kind and understanding with regard to me was this cousin, after I grew up and began to earn my living. He cannot have approved of my going, as a girl of twenty, to Paris to do journalistic work. Yet he helped me in every way open to him, and gave me introductions to many well-known people.

The centre of his life, as long as she lived, was his mother. After she became a widow, and lived more or less an invalid life, he occupied a small suite of rooms just beneath the *appartement,* close to the Bois de Boulogne, where she had moved a few weeks after her husband's death. Marcel was constantly with her, and was always ready to help her to entertain certain boring acquaintances, survivals of Uncle Charles' circle, all of whom he knew disliked him very much. He would put aside any engagement if he thought my aunt less well than usual, and the last time I was in Paris before her death, she said to me that God had been very good to her in giving her a son who was not only the most amusing and delightful of companions, but who was also always thinking of ways in which he could bring new interests into her life.

As is always the case, I think, with high-minded people, especially when one of them cherishes a profound love for the other, as time went on Charles and Lily Ballot had grown far more united than those who had known them in the first years of their married life would have thought possible. He became broaderminded, less opinionated, and even showed himself willing to receive the kind of people whose company she enjoyed, rather than that of those stiff folk among whom he had spent his youth. During the last years of their joint life they sometimes went to the south of France instead of to what Lily used to call, to my mother, *l'éternal St. Jean de Luz,* where, by his wish, they had always spent his legal vacations.

Not long before her death she wrote, and she was a very sincere woman,

"Were it not for my Marcel, I should welcome the end of my separation from Charles. Indeed I long for the moment when we shall find each other once more, this time at the feet of God, in a world where there will be no anxiety, no painful surprises of the sort time brings to us all, and when so much that has been obscure in this our life, will become clear."

VIII

I SHOULD be sorry indeed if the account I wrote of René Millet's disapproval of Paul Déroulède should cause any of my readers to feel prejudiced against a fine-natured human being for whom I have retained strong feelings of affection and gratitude. Had I had no better reason, I must have felt a measure of attachment for my dear Aunt Lily's eldest son. But the loss of his own father when he was six years old gave him, as I grew up, a feeling of pity for me, as well as considerable concern for my future. Being my godfather—one of my names is Renée—he regarded himself, in a measure, as my guardian.

Though he was quite unsentimental, and had a somewhat cold manner in everyday life, he began every letter he wrote to me with *Ma chérie,* and I now grieve I saw so little of him during my girlhood, for he was seldom in France. Being the manner of man he was, he strongly disapproved of my lack of a proper education, yet he was fond of my mother, and always showed her the greatest consideration and respect.

A shrewd student of human nature once wrote that every man dowered with generous instincts became, for a while in youth, an anarchist. To those who knew him in later life it was ludicrous to remember that phase in René's early life. It lasted only a short time, partly because he disliked, and even despised, the men with whom his then advanced opinions brought him in contact. And there was another practical reason why he soon put away what was, in truth, with him a childish thing. During the autumn and winter of 1870–71, the bitter cold, and even more the malnutrition he had endured as a very young private, so affected his health that for a time he was extremely delicate. Thus the question of how he was to earn his living caused acute anxiety to his mother. From thinking everything was wrong with the world, he had become as convinced a Republican as was his stepfather, Charles Ballot; but he had no liking for any of the men then composing the French Government. Such were also the views of the oldest and most distinguished of the Bellocs' family friends, Barthélemy Saint Hilaire, who had sacrificed to his opinions what might have been a brilliant career in diplomacy. It was to him René Millet, acting on the advice of our grandmother, Madame Swanton Belloc, at last went for counsel. Monsieur Saint Hilaire, who had known him from his birth, pressed him to apply for a prefecturial post. Those connected with the prefectures of France have always been regarded with respect, and for over a hundred years have played much the same part in the government of their country as do members of the British Civil Service.

René took the older man's advice and, owing to his having won the *Prix d'Honneur,* as the best all-round French scholar of the year 1867, he was appointed to what was then regarded as the pleasantest of French prefectures, that of Versailles. There he was stationed close to La Celle Saint Cloud, and we saw a great deal of him, I, as his little god-daughter, always obtaining a good deal of his notice and attention. This was a source of pride, but also sometimes of something like rebellion to the god-child, for *mon parrain,* as I always called him, had strange ideas as to the education and training of even quite small children. One of his theories was that every woman should be able to do what has to be done in her everyday life as well and as easily with her left hand as with her right hand. So when I was beginning to learn to write, my troubles were greatly increased by René's determination—and he was a very determined man—that I should write him a letter, every fortnight or so, with a pen held in the fingers of my left hand.

In that quite unlike my other cousins, who used to shower useless, delightful toys on me and on my brother, my young godfather always gave me something useful. I remember a silver thimble; an elegant tooled leather needle-case; and what really did give me pleasure, a tiny watering-can. On one exciting occasion he brought me a pair of miniature garden shears; but the moment he had left the house they were taken from me, lest I should cut myself or my brother.

When I was seven years old, I intensely longed for a miniature charcoal stove. I had seen one in the Bon Marché, and the price was fifty francs. That, as I sadly realized, meant it could only be bought by a millionaire, a decree the most foolish on the part of Providence, as obviously a millionaire's little girl would never be expected to do any cooking. And then a miracle happened! On the next New Year' Day, in the huge case Aunt Louise always sent her fatherless nephew and niece each *Jour de l'An* to England, was an even grander miniature charcoal stove than that I had so longed for, together with a *batterie de cuisine* to match. On that stove my brother and I used to make toffee, and now and again fry a couple of smelts.

My first clear memory connected with the Palace of Versailles was going to *goûter* with my godfather in a little drawing-room belonging to a suite of apartments situated in a part of the vast building not open to the public. René was staying with the Curator, and the tall windows of the room overlooked the rose garden where the luckless and vain Prince-Cardinal met, in the darkness of the night, the adventuress Oliva, believed by him to be Marie Antoinette. I was five years old, and this was the first time I realized the beauty of stateliness. Our *grand salon*, in spite of its name, had lost whatever stateliness it had once possessed when devastated by the Germans during the Franco-Prussian War.

After two years at Versailles, René Millet became the youngest sous-prefect in France, and was appointed to Saint Nazaire. The first letter he wrote after he was settled there was in English:

"My dear Aunt Bessie,—I present to you my best compliments and devotion, and beg to tell you how welcome you will be to my corner of Brittany. There you can enjoy sea-bathing, and also visit some curious remains of old France. I pray you to believe that apart from wishing to have the joy of seeing you, I long to offer you the attraction of sun and sea, which you will find sweet for the little ones. I beg you to believe in the affection of your truly devoted nephew, René Millet."

So ran the first of a great number of invitations; but want of money, and a curious dislike of staying away from whatever happened to be her home at the time, prevented my mother from ever accepting this sort of kindness. That was unfortunate for her children, especially as regarded René Millet's invitations, for he later had a long diplomatic career, and was posted to many countries.

It must have been about the time he was made a sous-prefect that his mother became aware her elder son ardently wished to marry his first cousin, Juliette Redelsperger. This would have brought great happiness to Aunt Lily, who dearly loved her niece. But Juliette felt René was like a brother rather than a lover, and comparatively soon, by a cruel stroke of fate, a friend of his, Étienne Siry, fell passionately in love with her, and their marriage soon followed.

Some time after the abortive—it cannot be called love—affair, with his first cousin, René Millet made up his mind it was time for him to marry and, mistakenly in my view, though he was prepared for his marriage to be arranged in the French way, he did not wish his mother to play any part in the matter. So it was through an elderly lady with whom he had become acquainted at Versailles, that he learned of the existence of a certain charming girl named Thérèse Urbain, whose mother was a sister of the noted scholar-academician, Gaston Paris. He was told the young lady was pretty, well educated, extremely amiable, and further that she fancied she would like to spend her life in the political world. René's elderly friend had a country house close to where Madame Urbain lived at Avenay, near Rheims, and invited René to spend there part of his leave. They were soon both asked to lunch by Madame Urbain, and it was then René revealed, for the first time, traces of what may be called the wayward Belloc temperament.

At lunch was also present the silent younger daughter of the hostess. Her name was Louise; she was only seventeen, and not nearly as pretty as her sister Thérèse. Yet there was something about her appearance—she was tall and slight, and all through her life she retained something of a fawnlike grace—which attracted René's attention, though he never even spoke to her during this first meeting. But after he had left the house he exclaimed, "Mademoiselle Thérèse is delightful, but the one I intend to marry is her sister!"

When this intention was conveyed to Madame Urbain, she firmly declared nothing would induce her to allow Louise to marry before Thérèse was settled in life. René on his side even more firmly declared he was quite willing to wait, the more so that he was certain he would not have to wait long, as Mademoiselle Thérèse was so very attractive.

And so it came to pass. Thérèse soon became engaged, and immediately after her wedding René asked to be allowed to pay his addresses to Louise. Then came the following letter to my mother:

"I want to tell you myself, dear Aunt Bessie, that I am going to be married. I adore my fiancée, and I hope you will show her

all kindness and sympathy. I have already spoken to her at length
of my English aunt, so she is longing to know you. I am beginning to understand two lines of Shakespeare, which I have remembered ever since I first read them:

> Ah me! how sweet is love itself possessed
> When but Love's shadows are so rich in joy.

I no longer live in the *shadows*, and it would make me very happy
if you and Marie would come to my wedding, and so take the place
of the uncle I have never forgotten, and for whom I cherished
so sincere an affection. I beg you to kiss tenderly for me your
children. I think you know how truly I care for them both, and
that I shall always be ready to do anything I can for either of
them. Believe in the respectful tenderness of your devoted René
Millet."

He spoke English well, and before the Franco-Prussian War,
he had had the good fortune to be asked on a long visit to Oxford, by a nephew of Maria Edgeworth, and that gentleman's
kind, hospitable wife. Their daughter is the only living human
being who now remembers my father, and I felt much moved on
receiving a letter from her, telling how, as a very young girl, she
had gone to La Celle Saint Cloud in the spring of 1867, and had
there seen both Louis Belloc and Bessie Rayner Parkes. She had
been taken for a walk by Louis and his mother in the woods then
carpeted with flowers. To Madame Swanton Belloc the name of
Edgeworth was specially dear, and I was taught, from babyhood,
to hold it dear, too.

Almost immediately after their marriage, René Millet and his
bride were offered by Barthélemy Saint Hilaire, who was then
Foreign Minister, rooms in the little palace on the Quai d'Orsay
which was fortunately spared when the communists burned so
many historic buildings. It was an auspicious beginning of the

young couple's official life, and, in spite of her youth, Louise Millet proved an excellent hostess to the many foreign and official people Monsieur Saint Hilaire was obliged to entertain. Indeed I think she was never so happy as during the first two years of her married life in Paris. The eldest of her four sons, Philippe Millet, was born in one of the fine eighteenth-century *salons* on the ground floor, the *salon* having been turned into a bedroom for the occasion.

My godfather's wife was unlike any Frenchwoman I have ever known. She was more like a refined Englishwoman of the aloof, slightly mysterious, late Victorian type. Her great-grandfather was known to have been a Frenchman, attached to the court of Louis the Sixteenth, who had fled to Russia early in the Great Revolution. He abandoned his real name and title for that of Urbain, which may have been his Christian name, and when, fifty years later, his only descendant came to France, the man kept the name of Urbain. To my mind, Louise Millet looked Russian rather than French, and her religion was not at all like that of the average Frenchwoman of her education and class, for it was strongly mystical in character. Several British diplomatists, during my youth, spoke to me with something like strong affection of my godfather, but not one of them ever alluded to his wife. It was a foreign ambasasdor who told me, years later, that an Italian had fallen so wildly in love with Madame René Millet that when he found he was going to another post *"il s'était tué pour elle,"* and this, having known her, I can well believe was true. She kept on good, but distant, terms with her husband's mother, and never became intimate with any member of the Belloc family. I felt her quite alien to myself, though I was exceedingly fond of her eldest son, who grew up into a man of outstanding ability and character.

Whenever the Millets moved to a new post, I always received a warm invitation from my godfather asking me to pay them a long visit. But my mother strongly objected to my leaving her. I was sadly disappointed when I was asked to Stockholm, where René was French Minister for some years; and I even more regret I never had a chance of being in Tunis, of which French colony René Millet was the first Resident General. I think his happiest term of official life was spent there. He was on excellent terms with Sir Harry Johnstone, who represented the British Government, and who in an official report, wrote a eulogy of the Resident General which gave my mother and me great pleasure.

René twice tried to "arrange" a French marriage for me. On the first occasion, during my stay as a girl of seventeen at La Celle Saint Cloud, he asked me, to my surprise, to a picnic. But I at once realized that this gathering had taken place that I might see, and be seen by, a young man who was distantly related to Louise Millet. Neither of us liked the other.

When I became engaged, some nine years later, my godfather felt much moved. He had been afraid I should never marry, as I had by then become what he—no one else—called a bluestocking. He wrote me several long letters containing his views as to the duties of a wife, and it came to my knowledge, long afterwards, that he had written to one of his English friends, asking him to find out everything he could concerning my future husband. Though far from a rich man, René gave me as a wedding gift a Persian lamb fur coat, and he also asked if I would like a dress made by his wife's Paris dressmaker or, alternatively, a roll of black silk. I foolishly chose the roll of black silk.

During the years that followed, he always found time to write me long, affectionate, intimate letters. And when my son was fighting in France, during the years 1917–18, the Millets put up, and hospitably entertained, not only my boy, but also one of his fellow officers, while he was on Paris leave. My godfather was then spending the last years of his life in the villa at Passy left him by Barthélemy Saint Hilaire. He was offered the Madrid

Embassy, but he refused it. This was a wise action on his part, for he would have been extremely unhappy away from his own country during the war.

As their four sons were all fighting from the August of 1914, René and his wife suffered agonies of suspense and fear. Yet, strangely enough, with the exception of Philippe, who was frightfully wounded at Charleroi, they all got through, though one of them, who was in the Navy, was twice torpedoed. I heard often from my godfather during the war, and his last letter expressed in moving terms his sorrow at the tragic news that my brother's eldest son, Louis Belloc, had been shot down in flames, almost within sight of the Armistice.

René Millet died suddenly in 1919. The eldest of his four sons wrote to me:

"You will understand, dear Aunt Marie, what a shock it was to all of us, and especially to me, who loved him so dearly, and to whom he was the best of fathers, as well as by far the kindest and most understanding of friends."

He was spared the anguish the premature death of the writer of that letter would have caused him. But how happy it would have made him, had he lived to old age as had done so many of our forebears, to learn that his eldest son's son, named René after himself, escaped from a German prison camp and, after a series of extraordinary adventures in Russia, joined the Fighting French. Another of his grandsons managed to get away from Africa in the June of 1940, disguised as a Polish officer, and is now flying in Syria. A distinguished diplomat, great-grandson of Gaston Paris, and so related to René Millet's wife, also belongs to what is now called *La France Combattante*.

IX

I CANNOT remember in which year of my girlhood I paid
my last visit to the château of Villebouzin which had been
bought by my uncle, Jacques Redelsperger, in the late fifties of
the last century. The château, which dates from the fourteenth
century, is not far from Montléry, and close to the village which
gives its name to what was for long a popular comic opera, *Le
Postillon de Longjumeau*. My aunt, who had fine taste, made it
delightful inside and out. They were devoted to the place, and
Uncle Jacques, *Ton-Ton*, as I and my brother called him, used
to go to Paris very early each morning, only coming back in time
for a rather late dinner, though this involved a comparatively
long train journey from Paris, and a drive of some miles.

In many ways Aunt Louise was far more like an Englishwoman, than a Frenchwoman, of that distant day. She enjoyed
entertaining all kinds of acquaintances, as well as friends, and
was always ready to welcome any member of the Belloc family to
Villebouzin. This was specially true of my mother and her children. We spent some weeks there each autumn, and to Hilaire,
as well as to me, the splendid old house was a kind of fairyland.
For one thing, the life led there was quite different from the quiet
life led at La Celle Saint Cloud. Very few strangers came to my
grandmother's house. Those who did were always English ladies,
and of them I felt slightly afraid, for I knew, by the exercise
of that sixth sense possessed by many children, that they were
almost always critical of me and Hilaire, and more especially of
me. It was natural they should regard my mother's little girl as

shockingly spoiled. I doubt if any of them had ever been in a French house where there happened to be children, so they were unaware that the average French child had no nursery, and pervaded his or her relations' sitting-room or study and, what was more surprising still, in those days, took all his or her meals, even late dinner, with the grown-up people.

At Villebouzin there was a constant coming and going of visitors whom I used to look at, and listen to, with eager pleasure, for from infancy I have been greatly interested in human nature. Jacques, the only son of the house, was full of farcical stories, and had a broad Rabelaisian humour which, if it shocked, always diverted, his listeners.

His sister, Juliette, was twelve years younger. I loved her dearly, and admired her manners and appearance, which was unlike those of her friends and contemporaries. She was quiet, gentle, and graceful. On her soft brown hair, dressed far more simply than was the mode of that day, she often wore a wide black velvet bow. I now know that her father, to whom she was all the world, wished her to recall the girls he had known in his youth, for he came, as his surname told, of Alsatian stock. Every day Juliette would give up a great deal of her time to amusing the children staying in the house, kind and unusual behaviour in a girl on the eve of womanhood.

Aunt Louise was the dominating spirit at Villebouzin. She kept a firm hand on everything that went on, indoors and out. Her strong, also Rabelaisian, sense of humour, was only equalled by that of her only son, and even to me, as a child, it was funny to hear her sharply rebuke him, after she herself had uttered what one of her guests would call *une énormité*, for saying something improper in the presence of Juliette's cherished governess, Miss Holt.

That lady was a stately-looking woman, who spoke very good French, and held her own in a way every one admired, and which few at Villebouzin could emulate, with the mistress of the house. But Juliette's governess was always treated as a guest, and a highly respected family friend. I was touched the last time I saw my aunt, when she was bravely dying of a painful complaint, to hear her speak with grateful affection of this Englishwoman. She said, with what I felt to be a touch of pathos, "Miss Holt has been, and will go on being, a second mother to Juliette."

I wrote that tribute to my mother, who, as I was well aware, had never much cared for the fellow countrywoman with whom she had so little in common and who, as even she must have realized, regarded the way I was being brought up, it cannot be said educated, with strong disapproval.

Not long before my last visit to Villebouzin, I became acquainted with a strange and terrible passage in the history of the château. My cousin, Marcel Ballot, who more or less guided me in my choice of French books, had strongly advised me to read the account, written by her confessor, the Abbé Pirot, of the last days of the Marquise de Brinvilliers. This narrative, which calls Defoe to mind, is one of the masterpieces of French literature, and within the last twenty years a distinguished Englishman told me that he partly owed his conversion to the Catholic faith to the fact that he had read that strange and most moving work. In the piteous portrait of the unhappy woman, which was drawn after she had been tortured, just before her execution, the abbé's face is seen dimly in the background.

Having read her confessor's account of his poisoner-penitent, I naturally went on to what was then a comparatively new book, *L'Affaire des Poisons*. There may be found the best and most vivid account of an event which occurred at Villebouzin two hundred years before my last visit. From the moment we drove up to the door of the château, my mind was possessed with what I now knew had taken place there in the private chapel which I suppose must have been destroyed during the Great Revolution.

In the hope of inducing the spirits of evil to restore the love of Louis the Fourteenth to the then aging Marquise de Montespan, a Black Mass was celebrated on the altar of the chapel, the celebrant being an infamous sorcerer-priest named Guibourg, who at one time had been private chaplain to the then owner of Villebouzin. The Mass was said on the Marquise de Montespan's naked body, as she lay on the altar, and, at the moment of the Consecration of the Host, the celebrant called on Ashtaroth and Asmodeus, styled by him "Princes of Friendship," to accept the sacrifice of the blood of an infant he had just killed.

A lady-in-waiting of the marquise was present at the Black Mass, and she later described every detail of what had taken place to the then chief of the French police, de la Reynie, and what she told him was later confirmed by two other people who had also been present.

Villebouzin had been chosen because the château was some way from the village of Longjumeau; there were no houses near it; and Guibourg happened to have kept in his possession a key of the chapel. As I wandered about the great, now almost empty, house, I used to wonder in which of the bedrooms the Marquise de Montespan had slept, the night before the Black Mass was celebrated.

I once read in a book of memoirs I have been unable to trace, what happened at the Palace of Versailles, immediately after this hideous ceremony had taken place in the private chapel at Villebouzin.

The King sent for his old friend, so as to bid her a solemn farewell in the presence of certain members of his Court who had been scandalized by their conduct. The Marquise de Montespan had meant much to Louis the Fourteenth, not only as lover, but as the mother of children he cherished; and some of those present at this penitential scene were ready to burst into tears at the sight of so sad a parting. But instead of bidding the marquise farewell, he took her hand, and walked firmly towards a door which led to an inner room which every one there knew was empty. After a while, the two reappeared, the King obviously as much in love as when his mistress had been young and extremely beautiful. In one of Madame de Sévigné's letters, written just afterwards, she said, "Their attachment seems stronger than ever. Indeed no one has ever seen such a return of love!"

But de la Reynie, who was a fearless man, had been put on the track of a nest of sorcerers, of whom Guibourg and his friend, the poisoner, Madame la Voisin, seem to have been the most potent and successful. Not only did they by their acts and incantations bring back love to the forsaken; they also provided the means by which women, tired of their husbands, achieved widowhood. It soon became plain to de la Reynie that providing secret poisons for the unwanted was their main business, and he put the facts and the proofs he had managed, with great difficulty, to procure, before the King. A full investigation was ordered. But when Louis the Fourteenth learnt that the Marquise de Montespan had long been a client of La Voisin and Guibourg, he at once suspended the inquiry, though, owing to de la Reynie, certain members of the court who had had dealings with these two people, were not only banished from Versailles, but imprisoned for life in fortresses far from Paris.

To go back to my last visit to Villebouzin. My mother and I made several expeditions in what was then a neighbourhood filled with curious and romantic survivals of old France. The most interesting of these survivals was only four miles from the château, and consisted of the ruins of what had been a very much grander place than my aunt's château. Indeed the buildings recalled an English castle. The man who had owned the property during the last half of the eighteenth century had been one of the *Fermiers Généraux* who, because of their wealth and power, were detested by the common people. His name was Berthier, and he was the first man guillotined in the Great Revolution. After his arrest, he was made to walk the whole way to Paris with a halter round his neck. What impressed us most in the now desolate park, was a vast depression which had once been a lake. There were long avenues branching out from its four corners, and there still stood statues on high pedestals commanding the depression formerly filled with water. We were told the lake had gone dry the night after Berthier was guillotined.

We also visited a most curious château which was evidently much older than Villebouzin. It stood perilously poised on the edge of a high precipice, and had not beeen lived in for many years. When I stayed, many years later, at Airlie Castle, I was strongly reminded of this French stronghold.

Uncle Jacques died when I was twelve years old, and though I had seen much less of him than of my other French relations, he impressed my childish imagination more than did any other of the older men among our relations. I must have been unconsciously aware of his powerful character. He was tall, fair, and very good-looking. He said little; but what he did say was always worth hearing and to the point. The only trait he had in common with his wife was an unusual generosity of nature.

At the time Louise Belloc fell in love with Jacques Redelsperger, he was a clerk in a stockbroker's office, and my grandparents did not regard the marriage as in any way suitable. For one thing, he admitted his lack of interest in art and literature, and all he then possessed in the way of capital was three thousand francs (£120) left him by his father. But Louise, highspirited, obstinate, always knowing what she wanted, was determined to marry him. Even as a little child she had been bold and fearless, always saying exactly what she thought. On one occasion her father exclaimed, *"Elle appellerait le Bon Dieu 'Pierrot'!"*

Louise Belloc and Jacques Redelsperger married on an income which even for those days was minute. But once they had accepted the young man as a son-in-law, the Hilaire Bellocs, kind and unselfish as they seem always to have been, built on part of their garden the chalet which became, in the autumn of 1867, my parents' first home. Louise did a great deal of her own housework, grew vegetables in her tiny garden, and went on with her painting. Even as a girl she had exhibited in the Salon, and though she was regarded, in that unlike her sister, as only an amateur, her pictures always sold.

When she knew she was going to have a child, she amused her parents, and shocked Mademoiselle de Montgolfier, by borrowing from some of Hilaire Belloc's pupils at what was then oddly called the Imperial School of Design, Mathematics, and Sculpture, certain Greek casts. These she placed about the little rooms of the chalet, in the hope her baby might thus be helped to the beauty she lacked. As to that she was disappointed, for Jacques *fils,* as he was called from the moment of his birth, grew up to have everything a man could wish for, excepting good looks. He was extremely ugly, reminding his English aunt of the famous portrait of Mirabeau, for his face was alive with intelligence. Had he not been the only son of a wealthy man who denied him nothing, he might have become either a successful writer or artist. As it was, he idled his life away, and ended by being the popular *boulevardier* of legend and of song.

At the time of their eldest child's birth, his parents were compelled to live all the year round at La Celle Saint Cloud, for they could not afford even a tiny apartment in Paris. Then, to the amazement of Louise and Hilaire Belloc, their son-in-law came back from Paris one summer evening, and going into their house, told them he had been made a member of the Bourse. He had found two sureties ready not only to testify to his high moral character and integrity, but also to make themselves responsible for a considerable sum of money, for no member of the French Stock Exchange is allowed to become bankrupt.

At once his happy wife bestirred herself to find a large and comfortable apartment in Paris. She chose one in the Boulevard de la Madeleine, and it was there that their only daughter, named Juliette after her father's mother, was born twelve years after her brother. Very soon Villebouzin and its splendours was acquired by Jacques Redelsperger, and brought happiness, health, and pleasure, to a large circle of relations and friends.

In his grave reserved way, Aunt Louise's husband was touchingly devoted to his wife's family. During the Siege of Paris his kindness to his sister-in-law, Lily Ballot, was constant and vigilant. The Ballots considered that they owed to him in a great measure their son Marcel's survival. The child was extremely delicate, and the question of feeding him during those months would have been an insoluble problem had it not been for his kind, generous uncle. Jacques Redelsperger also helped to keep alive Mademoiselle de Montgolfier and her devoted maid. After the two Belloc houses at La Celle Saint Cloud had been devastated in the autumn and winter of 1870–71, it was to her brother-in-law Aunt Lily turned for help, when she found her mother and my parents were determined to return there as soon as was possible. He at once bought furniture—then at a fantastic price—and arranged for certain rooms to be made habitable.

More fortunate than many others had been, the Redelspergers lost comparatively little during *l'année terrible,* for Villebouzin was turned into a hospital by the enemy. But of course the Prussians stole all the tapestries, the clocks, and the eighteenth-century furniture which had been collected with such pleasure by Aunt Louise. The few valuable pictures were always taken into Paris each autumn, so they remained in France, as did the collection of autographs, all letters written by famous women, which, strange to say, was Jacques Redelsperger's only hobby.

There had been no marriage settlement when Louise Belloc married, so, by French law, his widow inherited the whole of her husband's fortune. Yet, after her husband's death, she decided to sell Villebouzin. She had gone on caring more deeply for this silent reserved man than any one round her had believed to be the case during the later years of his life, and she no longer filled her country house, as she had done, during six or seven months of each year, for over thirty years. But I think she must have lived to regret she had sold the château, for she was the sort of woman who consciously enjoys the spacious life of a great country house. Still, though she was already stricken with her last illness, with characteristic energy and determination she bought and made attractive a house at La Celle Saint Cloud, close to the Sirys' property. There was a large studio in the garden, and she went on painting, and even sculpting, between bouts of dreadful pain, for she refused to have an operation which might have brought her relief. Though she spent more and more time in the country, she stayed for a few months of each winter near the church of Saint Augustin, seeing her friends almost to the last, and re-reading the books she had enjoyed. On the day she died, she read the last chapter of Dumas' *Le Collier de la Reine*. By her firmly expressed desire, my aunt was buried in her father's grave at Père la Chaise, instead of at La Celle Saint Cloud.

In an account of her sister's funeral, written by Aunt Lily to my mother, she said that they had all been surprised to see a number of unknown shabby men and women, to whom Louise had been kind, and who had come to do her memory honour. Lily Ballot ended her letter with the words:

"Louise, as a girl, was bitterly resentful of her lack of charm. Though she looked at life squarely, she would have been surprised to learn that in spite of her remarkable kindness of heart, it was her madly imprudent tongue which often banished all kind feeling on the part of her relations, as well as of her friends, and caused her at times to be almost hated.

"With the exception of our father, I knew her better than did any other human being, and I can honestly say that I cared for her during the whole of our lives with what was at any rate something of what should be a sister's affection. There were times when her habit of making mischief brought me real suffering—suffering which I resented, and thought most cruel, as coming from her to me. But one thing I feel I should tell you. She was always kind to our brother. What real love she was capable of feeling was concentrated on two men; our father, to whom she often showed what were, for her, most unusual marks of tenderness, and her son, Jacques. Jacques would be a better man had she loved him less, for she always spoilt him, was jealous of his liking for others and, at the very end of her life, she left him a far larger share of her fortune than was fair to her loving daughter, and to that daughter's children."

X

To go back to that first summer spent in France after I believed myself grown up. No doubt part of my happiness was owing to my being among people who had been attached to the group of men and women of whom I had retained such loving memories. In those days, the average French girl belonging to such a family as was my family, led a singularly serene and joyous existence, for all those about her tried to make her see life under the pleasantest auspices. Our straitened means, which had so affected my life in England, did not seem to matter, in a neighbourhood where all the pleasures open to young people were of a simple nature, and did not involve the spending of money, even on such an item as a pair of tennis shoes. The first French tennis court on which I ever played had been marked out on a piece of rough grassland, and in a space overshadowed by chestnut trees.

Thirty years later, when even in France almost every house had a telephone, it became easy for people to get in touch with one another. But such was not the case in the 'eighties; and yet, as is said to happen in the Far East, everything became known very soon. Within a short time of our arrival at La Celle Saint Cloud, men and women, especially women, began to write from Paris to say they would like to come and see me and my brother, as they had known our grandparents. In almost every case their names brought dim echoes of my childhood. A number of them had worked in my grandfather's studio, and one charming person, named Alice de Forestier, had come fairly often during the years that followed my father's death. When I saw her again, after ten or twelve years, I felt a shock at the change in her appearance. It made me realize for the first time that human beings alter as time goes on. I had always been accustomed to being with elderly people, and I had never become alive to the changes brought by the passage of the years.

There were also certain tiresome visitors I was glad to see, because they reminded me of the past. In England they would have been called bores. One such was a lady who, when my grandmother was alive, would arrive in the early morning, having left Paris at cockcrow, and stay till it was dark. She, also, had worked in Hilaire Belloc's studio; but she did him no credit, for, to my mother's distress, she was always pressing badly painted watercolours on every one in the house, including the maids. She had a violent dislike of the Jesuits, and to them she ascribed most of the misfortunes from which France had suffered since the days of Saint Ignatius Loyola.

Aunt Lily always avoided meeting any of these peculiar old friends. At last she explained her attitude to my mother—who thought such conduct strange and rather unnatural, for she herself suffered fools gladly, especially if they happened to be poor and lonely fools—by admitting that her husband had always been much irritated by these sort of visitors. Years later, I discovered that several of these people had received tiny pensions from my grandmother and Mademoiselle de Montgolfier. I discovered something else. This was that after the deaths of Madame Swanton Belloc, and of the friend for whom Aunt Louise had always had a strong dislike, Louise sought out these old men and women, and continued the pensions as long as they lived.

I think the only really happy hours spent by my mother when we went back to our French home were those spent by her when, accompanied by me, she went to Paris. After she and I had done whatever "chores" had been the excuse for going there, we would take an omnibus, and climbing up on what was called the *impériale*, make for some museum, church, or historical monument, she wished me to see. And, as had been the case in the London of my childhood, she would fill Paris with figures from the past. She was particularly fond of the Marais, that quarter, so little known to foreigners, which begins behind the great square of the Bourse, and which still consists of a labyrinth of narrow streets. It contains the mediæval square, La Place des Vosges, in a corner of which stands the house of Victor Hugo, carefully preserved as it was when he inhabited it. Of far greater interest, to my way of thinking, is the Hôtel Carnavalet, where Madame de Sévigné wrote the famous letters to her daughter whenever she happened, for the good fortune of posterity, to be in her town house.

My mother had first gone to Paris in the 'forties, and she had retained a clear memory of the many curious byways which after surviving from the Middle Ages, were to her indignation swept away when Napoleon III decided to build what may be called the Opera quarter. She had actually met an old lady whose father had been guillotined in the early days of the Revolution, when a guillotine had been set up in the Carrousel, just behind where the Tuileries then stood. I remember her giving me so vivid an account of what the Place de la Concorde had looked like before the Great Revolution, that I have never crossed that vast space without remembering all she told me. How, till 1789, it was like an ill-kept field, with trees and bushes affording hiding-places for thieves and footpads. She possessed all sorts of curious, out-of-the-way bits of information. Thus she had discovered that the guillotine in the Place de la Concorde was frequently shifted, and that, on the day of the execution of Louis the Sixteenth, it was moved close to the Seine, to enable those standing on the other side of the river to see the killing of a king.

She had a strong dislike of the boulevards of which the Parisians are proud, and when we had occasion to go to the old quarter, we only crossed the Boulevard Saint Germain. As for the rue de Vaugirard, of which she retained tender memories, for there she had spent two happy winters with my father after my birth, on looking back I can see she avoided ever going down what is still the longest street in Paris. The only thing she ever told me concerning the rue de Vaugirard was that Madame de Maintenon had lived there, when in the capital, with the children of the Marquise de Montespan, because the street was so remote from the Paris of the court.

Becoming acquainted with my French relations from quite another angle to that I had had as a child was delightful to me. I also became keenly interested in my forebears, and I have remained proud of the fact that I and my brother came, on my father's side, of a family of fighters. For nearer two hundred than a hundred years, the majority of the men of the Chasseriau and Belloc clans have been engaged in the noble profession of arms. War has ever been, for me, an everpresent reality. It had come to my beloved country when I was just two years old, and I fully expected it would come again, as indeed it did, not once, but twice, during my lifetime as a grown-up woman. But when I went back to the France of 1885, though all those of my relations who had been of an age to fight in 1870 had fought, there was no professional soldier among them. They would have been indeed horrified to learn that not only their sons, but their grandsons, would all grow up to fight France's hereditary enemy.

During the first summer we spent at La Celle Saint Cloud, and during the two years that followed, I was a great deal in the company of my first cousins, but when I went to Paris to do literary work I was too busy to see much of them. Of many of my other relations, especially those who were older than Aunt Lily, till 1885 I knew little or nothing. The majority of Parisians,

including many of the working class, always left Paris each summer for a country house, large or small, of their own. Also, in
what now seem to me such far-away days, the journey to and
from our village took nearly two hours and, for those who,
like ourselves, were compelled to be of frugal mind, was an expensive business.

I had retained a warm feeling of affection for my great-aunt,
Madame Bibron. She was the only surviving sister of my grandfather, Hilaire Belloc, and as to age, might have been his daughter. She outlived him by twenty-seven years, and was close on
ninety when she died.

There are still, though they are becoming rare, certain quiet
women who seem to play but a small part in the lives of those
about about them, and yet leave behind them a singular void
in the hearts of their friends. This was true of the small, white-
haired, silent being my brother and I called Tante Jenny.

To the Hilaire Bellocs, then newly married, had come Hilaire's
little sister on the death of her mother. They both loved her
dearly, and the only time when there came a small rift between
her brother and herself was when, aged twenty, she insisted on
earning her livelihood as a teacher of drawing in a Government
school for girls. Hilaire, being the manner of man he was, had
wished her to marry young, and lead the normal life of the
Frenchwomen of their time.

Though she was not good-looking, and had no *dot*, two of the
young men who came and went to what must have been a
pleasant cheerful household, asked her in marriage. But she
waited till she was thirty—even now, in France, a most unusual
thing. Then Gabriel Bibron, a young naturalist who was just
her own age, fell in love with her. She accepted him, and Aunt
Lily once told me she remembered the excitement and fun they
all had in furnishing the small *appartement* over the serpent-

house of the Jardin des Plantes. In those little rooms one of the two lovers was to live for sixty years. They were wonderfully happy for a short time; but poor Jenny's Gabriel soon developed tuberculosis and, till his death at thirty-seven, she was his devoted nurse. He must have been well thought-of in his own line, for, to my surprise, I once came across a short account of him in Larousse, and his widow was allowed to stay on in what had been an official residence.

Tante Jenny did not recall any other member of the Belloc family. Her fair hair had turned white when she was young, and she was small and thin. She had, however, fine dark eyes, and an expression of lively intelligence.

I lately found a letter she wrote to my brother when he was ten years old:

"I thank you, Hilaire, for your letter, and for the drawing which you sent me. I would like you to know, dear child, how much I love you. Firstly for your own sake, and also in memory of your grandmother, who so often used to talk to me of you and of Marie while you were in England. I also love you because you are the grandson of my brother, a man who was distinguished by his talents, by his devotion to his family and friends, and last, though not in any sense least, by his services to the country he loved so truly during his long arduous life. These, dear Hilaire, are your letters of nobility."

The letter does not end with any of the elaborate usual phrases of goodwill and affection so dear to the French heart. It is simply signed "J. Bibron."

Unlike my grandmother, and her daughter, Lily Ballot, Madame Bibron wrote few letters. But in the June of 1882, my mother received from her a letter so characteristic of the writer, that I give it:

"Dear Bessie,—I would like to tell you that not long before her death, my beloved sister—for so I always regarded her as being—begged me earnestly to cherish you, in memory of her affection and gratitude for the love and goodness you showed her son. And I venture to ask you, my dear niece, to request Hilaire and Marie to sometimes write me a few lines. They are both dearer to me than they know, if only as the grandchildren of my only brother."

And on the next page she addressed to my brother, then on the eve of his twelfth birthday, the following lines:

"Try and work steadfastly and constantly, my dear Hilaire, for thus alone is happiness to be found. In work, also, can only be found that tranquillity of soul which nothing can destroy."

With regard to work my brother has certainly followed this injunction. But a strain in the Bellocs of which I think Jenny Bibron remained unaware, though it undoubtedly came to them from her own mother, has denied him, as well as his sister, that tranquillity of soul their Tante Jenny believed to be the reward of steadfast and constant work. She herself was very active, and long after she was eighty she preferred to walk, rather than take an omnibus, when business or friendship brought her from the left to the right bank of the Seine. She much enjoyed showing the Jardin des Plantes, of which she knew, I am tempted to say, every tree, bush, and flower, to the children of her acquaintances. To the last she would also shepherd strangers who found themselves in that little known public garden, and if they happened to be naturalists, there would be no trouble too great for her to take on their behalf.

As time went on, each of her nieces often made an excuse to go and see her. With the elder of the two, Louise Redelsperger, all she had ever had in common was love for the man who had been the father of the one, and the brother of the other. But this formed a strong tie between them. Lily Ballot had been cherished by Tante Jenny from that delightful creature's birth, and the Ballots' was the only house in Paris where she would sometimes come to lunch and dinner after Madame Swanton Belloc's death.

Louise happened to be with her aunt when a clot of blood reached Tante Jenny's heart, and she lay back in her chair and died. As had been the case with both the sisters, Baronne Leroy and Baronne Habert, who were so much older than herself, and whom she so little resembled, Madame Bibron left strict injunctions that she was to be buried in the simplest way, and at the least expense. In place of a requiem, she desired a low Mass to be said at her funeral service. She had told Lily she wished no *faire-parts* to be sent out. But as to that her wish was not observed, for the men of the family considered such an omission would appear strange to their large circle. And so, as Lily wrote to my mother, what Tante Jenny had wished should not be done, in order to spare the niece she loved as a daughter the sending of answers to many letters of condolence, was done.

"My task was not made the easier owing to the majority of those who received the *faire-part* having never met Jenny, and knowing nothing about her. Several of them, indeed, expressed astonishment that any member of my father's generation should have lived so long. Do you realize, Bessie, that her death took place over a hundred years after the birth of her brother?"

To my great regret, Madame Bibron destroyed, before her death, all the letters she had received from Hilaire and Louise Belloc, as also from her two sisters. Of those elder sisters of my grandfather I know nothing, excepting that Mélanie Belloc, Baronne Leroy, had been very fond of my father, and had tried to arrange a marriage for him not long before he met my mother. As also the unusual directions each had left concerning her obsequies.

I had never seen the only survivor of the Chasseriau family, for during my childhood he spent at least six months of each year on an estate situated a long distance from Paris.

I now made the acquaintance and became fondly attached to both the Baron and Baronne Arthur Chasseriau. They lived in an old-fashioned *appartement* in the rue de la Néva, close to the Russian Church, and there I was always sure, as long as they lived, of a warm welcome in what was a true abode of love and friendship.

From when he was a little boy, Arthur had had a peculiar admiration and cult for his uncle, the painter, Théodore Chasseriau. Indeed, it is largely owing to him that Chasseriau has his place among the noted French painters of the nineteenth century. My cousin must have spent at least half his income in buying all those of Chasseriau's works which came into the market, and in sending his pictures, often to far-distant countries, to be shown in loan exhibitions. Every room in their Paris home, even the hall, was lined with Théodore's pictures and drawings. These included a number of family portraits, of which no engravings were made, for Arthur Chasseriau had what I think can be truly called the intense reserve which causes a very usual type of Frenchman and Frenchwoman to be averse from bringing any one of his or her name into undue prominence.

Not long before his death Arthur had the pleasure of arranging an exhibition of Chasseriau's work in the small gallery which stands in the Tuileries garden. I had the good fortune to be in Paris at the time, and I noticed what I think is known to few of those who admire this artist's paintings, the fact that he had another medium than oils, for there were then shown some fine water-colours. I am grieved I did not summon up courage to ask my cousin to give me one of these water-colours. As it was, he left his whole collection to the Louvre, where, according to rumour, it was immediately placed in one of the cellars.

Next to his absorption in his uncle—who had died at the age of thirty-seven, many years before the nephew was born—Arthur Chasseriau's principal hobby was genealogy, and he made out for me the Chasseriau family tree. I found it recently, and saw that my great-grandmother, Madame Swanton, had been the third child of a family of twenty, all by the same mother, consisting of sixteen sons and four daughters. Eight of the sons were officers of Napoleon; and, with the exception of the one who became a nun, each of the daughters married a soldier. Napoleon especially distinguished one of the eight brothers. His name was Frédéric; he had been born in the family house at La Rochelle in 1774, and was Chief of Staff to Milhaud, who commanded the French Fourth Corps of Cavalry at Waterloo. Baron Chasseriau led the great charge of the Cuirassiers, described by Wellington as the finest feat of arms he had ever witnessed. Frédéric left three sons, of whom the painter was one. Of the sixteen Chasseriaus, the great majority married, yet it is a singular fact that even when I was a girl I had but one relation of that name.

In a corner of the Baronne Chasseriau's *salon* was a curious kind of glass cupboard, on whose shelves lay dozens of military decorations won in battle by Arthur's grandfather, great-uncles, and two nephews killed in 1870. One day, when he was going over the collection in his glass cupboard, and telling me stories I ought to have written down at the time, he observed he did not keep there either his father's or his own Cross of the Legion of Honour, because neither of them had been awarded for a deed of valour. Arthur's father had held the peculiar official designation of *"Architect de la ville d'Algeer,"* and I remember my mother once saying to me, with a smile, that she thought our family ought to try and forget this fact, as the modern buildings in Algiers were, in her view, and she was often there before her marriage, staying with her dear friends the Bodichons, not only ugly in themselves, but quite unsuited to the climate.

As is so much more common with Frenchmen than would be believed in the English-speaking world, Arthur Chasseriau had cherished, from boyhood, a secret platonic love for the wife of the then Prefect of Algiers. Both her parents were English, though she had lived in North Africa all her life, and had married there. Without being at all pretty, she had great charm, was full of kindness, and extremely cultivated. Meanwhile, Arthur's parents were exceedingly anxious he should marry, and could not imagine why he refused to do so. When she was middle-aged, the lady Arthur had loved for so long became a widow, and after a time he asked her to marry him. She consented, and I have before me the modest *faire-part* in which they announced their marriage. It took place in 1884, just a year before I first met them, and when I saw them I erroneously thought them both very very old. Arthur Chasseriau remains in my memory as one of the happiest men I have known. His wife threw herself eagerly into all his interests, and never showed the slightest annoyance (as she might well have done) in his spending the greater part of their modest substance in promoting the fame of a man who had died some forty years before her marriage.

In my long life one of the things which has often irritated and angered me is the belief, so constantly expressed in England, that the French are so fond of money that they will do almost anything to procure it, and to keep it.

My cousin Chasseriau was a very average Frenchman; at no time of his life was he anything but a poor man; and I may perhaps be allowed to describe an outstanding occurrence in his later life, though he never spoke of it to my mother or to myself.

When de Lesseps planned the Panama Canal, French people in

every class of life believed it would prove another Suez Canal, and bring vast profits to the private investor. Time went on, and there came a day when, to his surprise and gratification, Baron Chasseriau was asked to join the Board, the emoluments being such as seemed likely to change the whole of his and his wife's life. But though no man of business, he very soon discovered that the company was in the hands of dishonest rogues. At once he gave up his directorship, and long afterwards he told my aunt, Lily Ballot, that he had gone through a time of wretched indecision as to whether he ought to make public what he believed he had found out. But he had had a painful interview with the already aged de Lesseps, during which he was assured all was to be made right, and certain men dismissed. These dismissals actually did take place. But three years later there burst on an astonished and wrathful France what remains in history as the Panama Scandal. Dozens of well-known men, especially politicians, were implicated. An inquiry took place; then a trial; and several of those concerned were sentenced to terms of imprisonment. But that brought little comfort to the thousands of small investors who lost their money.

I now turn to my recollections of a very different type of Frenchman, the scholar-statesman, Barthélemy Saint Hilaire. Although I was aware that certain members of my family did not care for him, I associated his fine austere personality with the whole of my happy childhood. I had also been dimly conscious of how devoted and faithful a friend he was of my beloved French grandmother. He used to take the long complicated journey from Paris, in order to spend two or three hours with Madame Swanton Belloc, at least once a week, and sometimes oftener. I propose writing a short account of my last meeting with him.

When I was twenty-one my mother and I spent together a few

days at La Celle Saint Cloud. Hearing from Aunt Lily we were there, he wrote and asked us to come and see him, so we made what was then a long journey by omnibus, from the Gare St. Lazare, to his villa in Passy.

I had never been to that quiet suburb close to the Bois de Boulogne, and my mother told me that when Passy was a village, Benjamin Franklin had lived there during part of his sojourn in France. She felt a lively interest in that many-sided American worthy. This was partly because he had been a friend of her great-grandfather, the scientist Joseph Priestley. One of the things which had made me as a child realize what distance means, was learning that when Franklin and Priestley played a game of chess across the Atlantic, each move took six weeks.

Barthélemy Saint Hilaire was eighty-six when we called on him that spring day, but he looked like a hale and hearty man of sixty. Though it was bright daylight, we found him in a curtained room, having just risen from a large writing-table on which stood a lamp which threw a pool of radiance where he had been sitting. He explained he had been advised, years before, by a German oculist, always to write in a strong artificial light. He put the fact of his having preserved his eyesight, to having followed this advice.

He invited me to sit down where he could see me clearly, and asked me to take off my hat. Then, as my mother wrote to Mrs. Rundle Charles on the next day, he said as if speaking his thoughts aloud:

" 'It is true that she is, in a sense, very like Madame Swanton Belloc. Indeed her head might be that of the lady I first knew when I was aged twenty-four, and for whom I cherished an affection and veneration which filled all my heart until the hour of her death.' "

There were not added in the letter the further words he had murmured in conclusion. These words were, *"C'est elle, en moins
bien."*

My mother was not only moved, she was surprised, to hear him
allude to what she knew had been a lifelong devotion on his part
to her husband's mother, for she had always found him extremely
reserved, and dry in speech and manner. I saw tears well up to her
eyes, and roll down her cheeks. He did not notice her emotion, for
she sat outside the circle of bright light.

Aware that Monsieur Saint Hilaire had never really liked her,
and had disapproved of her marriage, these facts had never
affected her kind feeling for him. Seeing him now had obviously
brought back a flood of memories. But the old man seemed hardly
aware of her presence, and he concentrated his whole attention
upon me.

To my considerable unease he closely examined me as to what
I intended to do with my life. When I told him I hoped to become
a novelist, he made no comment, but I felt he strongly disapproved. I feel sure he had never read any romantic literature written after 1800, and for many years his only living interest had
centred in international politics. I had heard how shocked he had
been to see lying on a table in our house a novel written by Zola
(I think *Germinal*) and how horrified to learn that my mother
and Madame Swanton Belloc had read the book with admiration.
No doubt he thought the English daughter-in-law had led his
dear friend astray. My mother understood him far better than he
understood her, and she had for him a sincere esteem. All the same,
she was amused when a lady tartly observed that his integrity
had won him the nickname of Aristides the Just. The lady's son-
in-law was a Senator, and she was irritated because Saint Hilaire,
if she was to be believed, was the only member of the Senate who
never availed himself, when conducting his private correspondence, of certain postal privileges.

He and my mother had always been, as to one thing, in full agreement. They both felt convinced that Germany was biding her time, and would again fall on France. He once told her that while he was Foreign Minister he had urged the country should be made ready for a sudden unprovoked aggression; he added that a certain frontier incident had caused him great anxiety. At the time he became Minister for Foreign Affairs, he was seventy-five, but full of mental and physical vigour, and he heard perfectly to the last day of his life. Perhaps because of his parentage, he seldom mentioned the Army, or engaged in talk concerning military affairs, but on one occasion, when spending an afternoon at La Celle Saint Cloud, he reminded Madame Swanton Belloc of how, in 1831, he had described to her and her husband a new secret gun. He held the view, which I now share, that in time engines of war will become so terrible that all human conflict on a great scale will end. In that connection he quoted Agesilaus and his catapult.

To return to our last meeting. As he talked on, I had an eerie feeling he was wafting me back into the past. I did not tell myself that seeing me now grown-up had recalled those days, so far away and long ago, when he was lonely, poor, and burdened with the knowledge of an illustrious paternity of which he was ashamed, and had suddenly found sympathy and kindness in the normal happy household of the Hilaire Bellocs.

Three years before my grandmother's death, when she had not been as well as she generally was, Barthélemy Saint Hilaire wrote to her younger daughter:

"I have been feeling anxious concerning your mother. I seem to know instinctively when anything is wrong with her. Even when I was quite young, indeed I may say when she and I were both young, for she is only eight years older than I, I experienced for her a feeling of veneration unusual on the part of a man for a beautiful woman. As the years went on, that feeling, that cult, became greater rather than less, and during my now long life, I have never met a man or woman with whom she could be compared as regarded nobility of mind and moral worth."

Madame Swanton Belloc, though she must have valued his unswerving devotion, did not share any of his opinions. She not only regretted, she could not understand, his admiration of Thiers, for whom she felt at times something like contempt. She was much amused when Gambetta, in one of his fiery speeches, called the old statesman "the serpent in spectacles." Yet the serpent in spectacles must have had a very human side, for my mother wrote about that time:

"There is certainly something very singular in the French character—something which is so at war with their logical and positive way of looking at life. I was astonished when Monsieur Saint Hilaire told me the other day that in the new house built by Thiers in the Place Saint Georges, he and his wife have reconstituted and furnished two rooms similar in every particular to the rooms which were inhabited by Madame Thiers' mother! They were destroyed by the Communists, and that is, he said, one reason why Monsieur Thiers looks back with such a feeling of horror at the Commune."

My grandmother was also quite out of sympathy with her almost lifelong friend's philosophical and religious ideas. She never concealed from him any of her beliefs. But each agreed to differ from the other, and when, during her widowhood, she was in any serious doubt or anxiety, such as that which filled her mind in the weeks immediately preceding the marriage of my parents, it was to this one man in her large circle she instinctively turned. Not that she always, or even generally, followed his advice. But, as she once wrote to her younger daughter, "Monsieur Saint Hilaire's views, with which I disagree, have cleared my mind, and have made me know where my duty lies."

I have found many allusions to Barthélemy Saint Hilaire in the letters Aunt Lily wrote to my mother during the four years which followed our visit to Passy. She saw him constantly, and though she had not liked him during her girlhood, for she was too intelligent not to know he must inwardly condemn the way in which she, her brother, and her sister were being brought up, she became, after her mother's death, really fond of him. He often called on her, and while she, too, disagreed with all his political and philosophical views, they had one subject on which they were in complete agreement. This concerned the manifold merits of her elder son, René Millet, to whom his old friend had become devotedly attached.

But René's half-brother, Marcel Ballot, never saw Monsieur Saint Hilaire if he could avoid doing so. "The sight of your great man's umbrella in the hall puts me to flight," he once told his mother in my presence; and I remember his saying that this family mentor and critic was the only human being of whom he ever felt afraid. Marcel was no doubt very well aware of how strongly the modern Aristides the Just must have disapproved of the petting and spoiling lavished by my dear aunt, after she became a widow, on her younger son. Love ruled her home, as it had done that of the Hilaire Bellocs fifty years before. Among the many things the old philosopher regarded as far better done in England than in France, was the caning of the boys in the great English public schools. He had a circle of attached friends in England, and often went to London for a few days, even after he was eighty.

And now I wish to put on record the following facts.

A few years after the death of Barthélemy Saint Hilaire, I was asked by the editor of an English review to write a paper describing the man and his career. But I soon found I was ignorant of what his life as writer, and later on as statesman, had been. All I knew of him, owing to a few words once said by my mother, was that he had been a son of the great Napoleon. And, as he had been dead some time, and had left no children, I considered myself entitled to reveal this curious piece of information. Instead of writing to René Millet (who was already, I think, Resident General of Tunis, and in any case away from France) as I ought to have done, I took the opportunity, when I was next in Paris, of calling on an acquaintance of my family. She was a writer of historical books, who I felt sure had known Barthélemy Saint Hilaire. Sure enough, she had known him well, and she went to some trouble to find out for me details of his long, arduous, working life. I then asked her to tell me anything she knew of his parentage. She said she believed he was the son of a Mademoiselle Saint Hilaire, who had apparently been, for a time, a mistress of Napoleon. As a young man Saint Hilaire described this lady as his aunt, and he had made his home with her until her death.

I embodied all that had been told me in my paper, and within a short time I received an indignant letter from René Millet, who had been not only Barthélemy Saint Hilaire's residuary legatee, but also his executor. He pointed out various mistakes I had made. Of these he said the most serious concerned the parentage of our old friend, and he asked who had told me what he called "a stupid story." He then revealed the truth, as told by me in a book concerning my own and my brother's childhood. The Mademoiselle Saint Hilaire described as his mother was, as a matter of fact, a sister of the officer who had been supposed to be his father. She had always believed him to be her brother's son, and when, after his mother's death, he had learned the truth, he did not undeceive her. That he had made his home with her for a time as a young man, was the only true thing in the account I had been given.

Although he did not actually put it into words, I felt, when I re-read his letter, that René Millet was shocked and sorry I had re-vealed the fact that Napoleon was Barthélemy Saint Hilaire's father. I think René was unaware of how widely this fact was known, though I never saw it stated in print until I had written my account of him in an English review.

Saint Hilaire only once spoke to Madame Swanton Belloc of his parentage. He then told her he had seen Napoleon twice, each time when he was nine years old. He was taken, with some other children, to the review held in the Carrousel shortly after the Em-peror's triumphant return from Elba. An officer of the Guard lifted the child on his shoulder, and all his life that child recalled the usually pale face flushed with emotion caused by the wel-come he had just received from his old officers.

The second time his unknown son saw Napoleon was a fort-night before the battle of Waterloo. The Emperor was pacing up and down the terrace of the Tuileries, his arms crossed, his head bent on his breast. On that occasion, none of the many people passing back and forth below the terrace even glanced up at him.

XI

I HAD long known that a friend of my father, named Anatole Dunoyer, was my own and my brother's legal guardian. But I had never seen him, and knew absolutely nothing about him. This, in a sense, was strange, for he had a house at Versailles where he, his wife, and their many children spent each summer.

I have only recently found an envelope inscribed by Madame Swanton Belloc "rough draft of letter to the guardian of my Belloc grandchildren." The draft is dated twenty-ninth of August, 1872, that is exactly ten days after my father's death. Monsieur Dunoyer and his wife had evidently been present at his funeral, for my grandmother alludes to having recently seen them. She states that the little property at La Celle Saint Cloud had been legally given over to his son by Hilaire Belloc, and that therefore my brother and I were now the owners of both the chalet and the house. She further gave details of the small amount of money left by my father, and went on to explain that our mother, his widow, had recently come in for a substantial fortune. She explained that an inventory of the contents of the two houses was being made, and would be ready by the time the meeting took place to which Anatole Dunoyer, as the guardian of fatherless children, would shortly be summoned. I have no record of when that meeting took place.

When I was eighteen, my mother suddenly told me she thought it time I made my guardian's acquaintance, and so, if I were willing, she proposed to ask him and Madame Dunoyer to receive me in their Paris apartment for a month.

I had been fascinated by the odd, violent character of Charlotte Princess Palatine, sister-in-law of Louis the Fourteenth, and
finding her life had never been written, I decided to write it. I
had begun the book during our stay in France the year before,
and when I came next to London, Dr. Garnett gave me a life ticket
to the British Museum Reading Room. So during my brief visits
to my godmother, Mrs. Pitt-Byrne, I used to work there. But I
was aware that any original and unpublished material of the kind
I required must be, if anywhere, in the French historical archives.
So I was overjoyed at the thought of being in Paris for a whole
month, though I remember wondering whether my aunts would
not think it strange I should be sent to strangers, rather than to
them. However, all new experiences have always been eagerly
welcomed by me, and I knew I should work very much better
staying with the Dunoyers, than with either Aunt Louise or
Aunt Lily.

I then learned the following facts concerning the man my
father had selected to occupy what would have been a position
of great importance in my own and my brother's lives, if our
mother had died while we were still children.

My guardian's legal name was Dunoyer de Segonzac, and his
grandfather, the Marquis de Segonzac, had been guillotined.
When he and my father were boys, he had always been called de
Segonzac. By the time he was twenty-one, he had become a strong
Republican, and decided to call himself plain Dunoyer. From
early youth he had occupied various important posts in the legal
side of the Republican administration, and had enjoyed for many
years a considerable salary. But when the French Government
decided to expel from France all the members of the House of
Orleans, he had felt revolted by what he regarded as an act of
gross injustice, and had resigned his high legal appointment.

As he was a man of high character and considerable attain-
ments, his resignation had made some stir. My aunt, Lily Ballot,

and her husband, though themselves so punctilious on what they would have called a *point d'honneur,* thought he had acted both rashly and foolishly, the more so as Madame Dunoyer was a delicate woman, and they had many children, who ranged in age from nineteen to four years old. His action had plunged his wife and family from what had been affluence, into something like real poverty. However, even if he had wished to do so, which he certainly did not, there could be no going back. So he had sold his house at Versailles, and had obtained a small position in a firm which published legal publications and books. He and his wife now intended to spend the whole year in what had been their Paris winter quarters in the Île Saint Louis.

All these facts my mother had lately learnt from Aunt Lily, and she told me that in the letter in which she was asking the Dunoyers kindly to accept me as their guest for a month, she was offering our guardian a hundred francs a week, which she thought would be, even if only for so short a time, a welcome addition to their much diminished income.

Monsieur Dunoyer sent a cordial reply, stating it would be a pleasure to have my father's daughter under his roof, and Madame Dunoyer wrote to me at the same time, saying she hoped her children and I would become real friends.

Meanwhile, I had gathered my mother had not much cared for the man who had been appointed our guardian, for she had no sympathy with the *doctrinaire* type of Frenchman. Also, his friendship with my father had been that of opposites. Madame Swanton Belloc, however, had always had a very high opinion of Anatole Dunoyer. That her opinion was justified was shown by what, after all, had been a noble decision.

So off I went, travelling alone to France for the first time, and filled with excitement at the thought of meeting a friend of my father.

There were certain parts of Paris with which I was very familiar; this was specially true of the streets situated in the Madeleine quarter, near the Louvre, and the Champs Élysées. I knew little of the left bank, no doubt in a measure because my mother shrank from going to a part of the town where she had spent the happiest days of her short married life. Still, we sometimes made a pilgrimage to Saint Sulpice, where my grandparents had been married, and we also went, from time to time, to the Luxembourg Gallery—for she much admired certain of the nineteenth-century French painters. But years went by before I visited the Sainte Chapelle, the Panthéon, and the Cluny. Of the Île Saint Louis I knew nothing. Indeed I had never been there, before the late afternoon when I arrived at the large eighteenth-century house where my guardian and his family occupied one of the higher floors.

Up to 1940 the Île Saint Louis was one of the few parts of Paris where a large and delightful apartment could be obtained for a low rent. The island remains like a corner of provincial France, and appears exceedingly quiet and remote from life as led beyond the bridges connecting it with the mainland. The views of the Seine, and of the banks of the river as seen from there, are most beautiful.

I ran up the wide shallow staircase, and the front door of the *appartement* was opened by a lad of eighteen, who greeted me effusively, and led me straight into his father's study. Anatole Dunoyer was a tall spare man with a fine head. His expression was severe, and he looked worn and sad. I at once felt for him a great respect, mingled with a certain awe. He belonged to the austere, silent type of Frenchman, and I know, now, he must have been at the time profoundly unhappy, for none of his friends, and above all none of his old political associates, had sympathized with what had been if a quixotic, a most rash, action.

After he had spoken to me at some length of my father, he examined me searchingly as to the historical book my mother had told him I was writing, for she had made this work of mine the excuse for wishing me to make a stay in Paris.

He then took me into the large sitting-room where his wife and children were all gathered together to welcome the stranger. Although Madame Dunoyer's eldest son looked grown-up, she had an astonishing appearance of youth, for she was small, slight, and might have passed for a girl. There was a daughter a year older than the son, and a number of younger children. Monsieur Dunoyer left me with them all, and I was taken to my room, which I later discovered had been, till my surprising visit, the one place of quiet and refuge of the eldest daughter. Madame Dunoyer helped me to unpack, and then we all trooped in to dinner.

I can still see the long narrow table, very like an English refectory table, on which stood at each end, and it was this which attracted my attention, two immense platters, heaped up high with thick slices of bread.

When we had all sat down, one of the children went and told her father dinner was served. I was placed exactly opposite to him, and after we had each had a plateful of potato soup, before any one else was served, he and I were each given a good helping of meat. For every one else, the meal consisted of a salad, and of bread and butter.

It is difficult for me to find words to express the astonishment I felt. The normal dinner then served each evening in a bourgeois household of moderate means would have consisted of soup, some kind of meat, poultry, or fish, a vegetable cooked in butter, and if no sweet was served, one of the many cheeses for which France was rightly famed. A good-sized chicken then cost three francs fifty, half a crown, and river as well as sea fish, was cheap and delicious. Meat was supposed to be dear, but there were many quite cheap cuts. Although I was not then aware of it, one reason why I so enjoyed my visits to France was owing to the well-cooked food served in the cheapest restaurants. Those were the days when an excellent meal could be enjoyed for about three francs at every Duval restaurant; and there were sixty Duvals in Paris. At many restaurants could be obtained a far cheaper meal than at a Duval, and every *marchand de vin* served at least one dish which was well, and appetizingly, cooked.

Monsieur Dunoyer left home each morning at eight-thirty, and he always lunched out. The egg dish, which had been the first course of every *déjeuner* I had ever eaten in a French private house, was served to me alone. This naturally made me feel very uncomfortable, and I earnestly begged Madame Dunoyer to allow me to live exactly as she and her children lived. She smilingly refused, her reason being that English people were used to substantial meals. So special food was cooked for me in the middle of each day, and three times a week my guardian and I had meat as part of our dinner. On Sunday, at midday, there was always a leg of mutton, and every child, even the youngest, was given a little bit.

Madame Dunoyer had entirely approved of her husband's action; and from having been mistress of a well-ordered house, with good servants to help her in the task of bringing up a large family, mostly consisting of boys who were clever, self-willed, high-spirited, and somewhat unruly, she found herself left with one old woman, who had been her children's nurse. This woman did the cooking, and everything else in the large *appartement* was done by Madame Dunoyer and her eldest daughter. The cook did what marketing there was to do; but this was easy, for, within a few yards of where we lived, through the centre of the Île Saint Louis, there ran a narrow mediæval-looking street lined with small shops.

It gradually came to my knowledge that the mother of the family only sat down when in the dining-room, and each evening, after dinner, when she always had by her side a large basket of household mending. She began each day by going to Mass at six o'clock. Then she came home, and gave her husband, and the boys who went off, it seemed to me unnaturally early to school or college, their breakfast of *café au lait* and bread.

Her grown-up daughter was the only French girl I had ever met, in those days, I felt to be unhappy, and I naïvely wondered why. I tried in vain to make friends with her, but she kept me at a distance.

As for me, I at once began working very hard, not only on my book, but also in trying to write articles on French subjects for English papers. So I was out of the house for a good many hours of each day and, to the evident distress of Madame Dunoyer, I often lunched at a Duval near to wherever I happened to be, instead of going back to the island. But one day I came in unexpectedly early, and I noticed the eldest girl standing still, looking out of one of the windows. It was so unusual to see her doing nothing, that I felt surprised. I suppose she thought that the person who had come in was one of her brothers, for she turned her head suddenly, and I saw tears rolling down her face. I felt greatly distressed, and rushing towards her, I asked her what had happened? Brushing the tears from her eyes with her hand as she did so, she murmured in a stifled voice, *"Maman se tue"* ("Mamma is killing herself"). I felt a sudden agonized shock of shame at what had been my lack of perception, for I realized what she had just said was indeed true.

I went into my room and sat down, feeling exceedingly troubled. After that day I began doing all I could to help Madame Dunoyer, especially with the younger children, whom I could sometimes keep quiet by singing them English songs, and some of my old nurse's Moody and Sankey hymns. The eldest daughter and I began to get on better. I think she felt grateful I had said nothing in answer to that pitiful cry of fear.

The four weeks went quickly, for I enjoyed my work, and I

became very friendly with my guardian's eldest son. He even wrote me some verses which I have always kept. He passionately wished to be a painter, a desire with which his mother secretly sympathized, but which his father regarded with strong disapproval. However, in the end, he had his wish, and those interested in modern French art are familiar with his work.

I became warmly attached to Madame Dunoyer, and sometimes I used to get up at five-thirty and go with her to Mass. This was the only time of the day she was ever able to be out of doors. She was not only cheerful, she was light-hearted and gay in manner, and used to ask me eager questions concerning the various members of my French family, for whom she seemed to entertain a touching cult. I remember how much I wished she could have made a real friend of my Aunt Lily, who would have shown her such sympathy and understanding.

I saw very little of my guardian, and although he always came into the *salon* after dinner each evening, I had become infected by his sons' fear of him. He would examine them closely as to their school work, and I never heard him utter a word of commendation or praise. While listening in silence to the shrewd questions and nervous answers, I contrasted in my mind the way my cousins were treated by their fathers, and I pitied the boys with all my heart. Not that they pitied themselves, for when out of their father's sight, and when he was out of the house, they would laugh uproariously, sing at the top of their voices, and tell us absurd stories of their adventures at school and in the streets. In spite, or perhaps because, of their very simple fare, they were fine-looking boys, full of vitality and high spirits.

There came the last day of my stay with those who had, in their varying ways, all become dear to me. My guardian stayed in that morning, and called me into his study. He began by expressing what he called his happiness at having come to know well my father's daughter. Having said this, he took from a

drawer an envelope addressed to my mother, and said hesitat-
ingly, "Be careful of this, my child." As I had learned, to my
mortification, he regarded me as unbusinesslike and careless, and
now he took out of the envelope the letter he had written to my
mother. Folded in it were the four one-hundred-franc notes she
had sent him, after he had written to say he was glad she had suggested my coming to stay with them for a month. With a smile he
observed it had been a most kind thought of my mother to send
him this money, but he was sure I would understand, now that I
had come to know them all so well, he could not accept the gift,
though he was none the less grateful to her for having thought
of it.

I never saw any of them again. What her daughter had said
was all too true. Madame Dunoyer died soon after my stay on the
Île Saint Louis, and years later, just after I had come back from
my ten days' honeymoon, I received a piece of old French silver,
with a sheet of paper on which was written: "*A Madame Marie
Lowndes, souvenir d'un vieil ami de son père, A. Dunoyer. Paris.
14 Janvier, 1896.*" And twenty-two years after what had become the cherished memory of my stay on the Île Saint Louis,
came the notification of my guardian's death in what is the longest *faire-part* in my possession.

There they all were—the many children, now grownup, with
whom I had once been thrown into such intimate contact. Each
of the girls had married; every boy had "made good"; and the
only one among them whose profession, that of artist, was not
inscribed in their father's *faire-part,* had become the most successful of the flock. I could not help feeling amused to note that
one and all of them described themselves as Dunoyer de Segonzac, as they had the right to do; and it is as de Segonzac the
painter has made his name. From Anatole Dunoyer's *faire-part* I
learnt, for the first time, of the various high offices my guardian
had held in the early years of the Third Republic. He died in his

eighthieth year, fortified, I confess to my surprise, by the Rites of Holy Church.

I was only with them for twenty-eight days, yet after fifty-five years, I often think of them, especially of the gentle, kind, serene mother. And, at times of my life when anxious about money, fearful of the future, and wondering what would befall my children—this was specially the case during the last war—I have found comfort and hope remembering that noble selfless Frenchwoman, and the gallant way she faced what must have been an almost intolerably wearisome, as well as a fearfully tiring, life.

XII

AND now I come to a time which was to bring great changes in my life. The small house in Great College Street, Westminster, of which the lease had been left to my mother by her uncle, had been let for many years. But in 1887 it became empty; we secured a tenant for our house in Sussex; and my mother decided to spend the autumn and winter in London.

I was then in my twentieth year, and apart from our neighbours in Sussex, my godmother Mrs. Pitt-Byrne, and Mrs. Rundle Charles, with each of whom we occasionally spent a few days, I knew no one in England. At Coombe Edge, Mrs. Charles' house at Hampstead, I had met men and women well known in the worlds of philanthropy and liberal politics, but none of these ladies and gentlemen had felt any interest in the kind of girl I was. Before her marriage, my mother had had a large circle of friends and acquaintances, and she now tried to get in touch with some of them. But her change of religion in 1864, and her marriage to a foreigner, had chilled their liking and affection, and though we saw certain well-known Londoners now and again, it never occurred to any of them to bring me in contact with young people of my own age. The only person I remembered with affection and gratitude was Madame Bodichon, and she had become an invalid, and lived in the country. But I was overjoyed to be in London, where I firmly intended to earn my own living by writing.

In those days, and for long after, Great College Street, though literally within a stone's-throw of the Houses of Parliament, was almost entirely composed of lodging-houses. Indeed there were only three private residents. These were my mother; our doctor, whose pretty house became fifteen years later the home of Lord Frederick Hamilton, a dear and delightful friend of my early married life; and the third, who lived in far the largest house, belonged to the Freemans, an old Westminster family. They were friends of Walter Besant, who placed there the scene of one of his early novels.

The street consisted of a row of small, early-eighteenth-century houses, and each little room had a high ceiling, and was of charming proportions. Opposite our house was (and still is) the oldest wall in England, apart from the Roman walls. Till 1800, London rose a foot a century, and the peaceful garden where Benedictine monks once walked and read their breviaries, is at least twelve feet below the level of the street.

When we had lived in Great College Street during my early childhood, Lady Augusta Stanley had lent my mother a key to the Abbey garden, and I remember distinctly running about the wide lawn, when I must have been about four years old, with a little bag of salt in my hand, trying hard and earnestly to put a pinch of salt on a bird's tail. At that time no one ever walked there, and the two singularly ugly houses which now deface it had not been built.

Twenty-five years went by before I was once more in that delightful garden. I was about to have my second baby, and the then Dean of Westminster most kindly gave me a key, thus enabling me to enjoy the good Westminster outdoor air without having to walk as far as St. James's Park. When he and his wife were translated—I must hope to a better place, though not to one more beautiful than was, till it was bombed and burnt, the Deanery—I was asked to return the key.

My mother was aware I wished to be a writer, and she again made a real effort to get in touch with various men and women she had known in her youth. I recall our going to Windsor to see Mrs. Oliphant. I much admired and still much admire certain of that writer's books, especially *The Beleaguered City*. But she must have regarded my expression of this admiration as impertinent, for in her autobiography there is a plain and indignant allusion to my having dared to do so.

Mrs. Lynn Lynton, who lived in Queen Anne's Mansions, close to Great College Street, was always kind to me; and we called on a son of Dickens who was then editing *Household Words*. But when consulted as to what would be the best way for me to begin my literary life, each and all of them, including Mrs. Charles, did their best to dissuade me from following in their footsteps, and earnestly assured me that far too many books were being written.

There was, however, an excuse for the way I was discouraged by these men and women. Those of them who had renewed their acquaintance with my mother were appalled by her daughter's lack of ordinary education. I spelt badly, both when writing English and French. I still do. The one subject I can truly say I knew far better than other girls of my age was English literature, for I had been a continuous reader ever since I had learned to read. I remember a man, afterwards Lord Courtney, asking me, in a jeering tone, the names of my favourite authors. When I replied "Defoe and Blake," he expressed surprise that I had ever heard of either of them. I discovered that he knew practically nothing of Blake, and that his idol was Tennyson, of whom I, on my side, then knew nothing.

Fortunately for me, I did not care what the people my mother consulted thought. What made me sad was that I saw she on the whole agreed with them, for she was afraid my lack of the sort of knowledge which had been instilled into all my contemporaries would make it impossible for me to earn a living with my pen. My brother was already writing remarkable verse.

A poem written by him at that time of his life has remained among his best work. He, also, was discouraged by my mother's literary friends; indeed two editors to whom she sent some of his verses wrote that in their opinion Hilaire Belloc would never become either a poet or a prose writer. But with that verdict she did not agree.

The memory of how I was then treated, no doubt with the best of intentions, has influenced me all my life in my treatment of would-be writers. I have always encouraged those who came to me for advice as to a literary career, and I have given, I can truly say, innumerable letters of introduction to publishers and editors. It seems to me obvious that with regard to any form of writing, a person either has or lacks the gift. There is no middle way, and the would-be author, even when vain and self-satisfied, very soon finds out if he has no chance of publication. The art of writing, even on the humblest level, cannot be acquired. This is naturally more true of creative work that of any other.

One day I went to see Cardinal Manning. From when I was a child he had always taken an interest in me though, as I grew into womanhood, he disapproved of what I may call my gaiety of nature. I was then very fond of dancing, and he thought every form of dancing wrong. I was devoted to the theatre, and had he had his way, no girl would ever have been taken to a play. He did, however, listen most kindly and sympathetically when I confided to him my wish to become a writer, and he gave me an introduction to W. T. Stead, who was then editor of the *Pall Mall Gazette*. Almost at once, Mr. Stead asked me to become part author of a guide to the Exhibition which was to be held in Paris in 1889, exactly a hundred years after the Fall of the Bastille.

My mother did not wish to go abroad just then, so I was sent to Paris, in the autumn of 1888, with Mrs. Mew, the woman who had become the nurse of her children fourteen years before. Nurse had proved her love for us, and her sterling worth, through our hard and difficult years, and though she had made me very unhappy as a child, I was by now much attached to her.

I was offered what seemed to me the enormous sum of ten pounds a week. I sent half to my mother, and Nurse and I lived on the balance in a small cheap hotel, on the left bank of the Seine. With me in the work was associated a clever journalist; but he had already laid the foundations of the guide, so after a short time he left France, and I carried on alone. Two pieces of good fortune soon befell me. The first was a meeting with Robert Harborough Sherard. A great-grandson of Wordsworth, to whom he bore a striking resemblance, he had drifted into journalism after leaving Oxford, and at the time was Paris correspondent of some great New York paper. He and his beautiful young wife were most kind to me, and after a while I persuaded my mother to recall Nurse, as they had asked me to be their paying guest. I lived with them for some weeks, and Bob Sherard helped me in every possible way, both as to my work on the guide, and with regard to the articles which I was now and again asked to write.

When he was invited to represent certain British trade papers, he not only handed the work to me, he also put me in direct touch with the editors in question. I especially remember writing an article describing all the tobacco shown in the Exhibition. These trade papers paid very well, and I was glad indeed of the extra money. As for the other ways in which this kind and generous friend helped me, I recall a commission to write an article which was to be called *Chez Robinson*. I had never even heard, till then, of that celebrated haunt of pleasure. To the French, Robinson Crusoe has always been a familiar friend, and *Chez Robinson* was supposed to recall this beloved hero. I remember bursting out laughing, to Bob Sherard's surprise, the first time I went to *Chez Robinson*, on thinking what Defoe would have felt if he had been taken there and told his book had inspired the vast playground. One of the features of Robinson's were little rooms built in the trees; and there were many side-shows which were supposed to recall a desert island.

I wrote a poor, pedestrian kind of article, soon to be transformed by Bob Sherard into what it ought to have been. I still remember the first line written by him. It ran: *"Chez Robinson, where the living is very high, and the thinking more than plain."* This was a perfect description. Indeed we might have left it at that.

My second piece of good fortune was of a very different nature. A first cousin of my mother, Aubrey Bowen, who had been treated as a son in her parents' house, had gone to Australia in early youth. There he had become, in due course, a distinguished oculist, and he had married a woman of great wealth. In 1889, the Australian Government had chosen him to represent them in Paris. He was a Unitarian, a man of the highest integrity and worth, and was devoted to the then invalid wife he had left in Melbourne. I now realize Cousin Aubrey much feared it might come to Mrs. Bowen's knowledge that he was being seen about in Paris with a girl. So, to my real chagrin, though he often gave me tickets for official receptions and other affairs to which he had no wish to go himself, he always refused to take me to any of the banquets which would have been, from my point of view, such fun. I stupidly thought this both unkind and inexplicable. However, he not only did whatever he could do for me during these months in Paris, but when he died, some years later, he left me an annuity of a hundred a year; the entire rest of his large fortune being devoted to the foundation of scholarships.

This legacy proved of inestimable benefit to me, for after my marriage—we were always happy, though often very anxious about money—I was able to raise a considerable sum on my annuity, and this eased our life for some years. Though I have gone on paying interest on the thousand pounds I then raised for nearly fifty years, I have never felt even a twinge of regret for what I did then.

To come back to my first real working visit to Paris.

All through my early childhood, my girlhood, and what had become brief visits to La Celle Saint Cloud, I had only known members of my French family and their friends. My mother, owing I think largely to want of means, had not kept up with certain noted French people she had known before her marriage. Also, after my French grandmother's death, we only paid flying visits to France, generally with a view to trying to let our houses at La Celle Saint Cloud. But I read a great deal of French, even while we lived in Sussez, and I was familiar with, and much admired, the work of such men as Alphonse Daudet, Maupassant, Pierre Loti, and Anatole France, to give the names of but a few. I little thought that I would ever have the chance of meeting any of these writers face to face; and while I was working in the Exhibition I had no time to think of anything else.

But when again living in London, I became exceedingly anxious to spend some time of each year in France; and though I soon began working for the *Pall Mall Gazette,* and other papers and magazines, I was always trying to think of good reasons for going to Paris.

Fortunately for me, though all the English daily papers had able correspondents there, there was an opening for lighter work than fell within these gentlemen's province; and I soon found that certain magazine editors were interested in French literature, French art, and even in French science. This gave me my chance, and now and then I would go off for a week, or even a fortnight, with perhaps between fifty and a hundred pounds' worth of commissions.

Meanwhile, I had been fascinated by the famous diaries of the de Goncourts, and foolishly, as I now know, I thought it would be well worth while making a selection from the many volumes for those readers, in England and America, who knew no French.

By this time I had become wiser, though not very much wiser, from what may be called the business point of view. So before starting what even I realized would be a long piece of work, I secured a commission to do the book from Mr. Heinemann; and the next time I went to Paris, I told my cousin, Marcel Ballot, what I was about to do.

He said I was undertaking a heavy task; also that Edmond de Goncourt, the survivor of the two celebrated brothers, was an ill-tempered man, and might cause me a great deal of trouble. However, I thought I knew best and, with his usual kindness, he gave me an introduction to de Goncourt, and also wrote to him.

Off I went to Auteuil, a Parisian suburb where I had never been before this, to me, memorable day. In spite of what Marcel had said, I was kindly received by the able old man, who could not conceal his astonishment that a girl should have read certain of his books, as also the fact that the one of his novels I most admired was *Germinie Lacerteux*. He was also surprised and pleased to note my pleasure in his collection of drawings by the great eighteenth-century French painters. They had been bought by him and his brother at a time such drawings cost less than did the lithographs of these same painters' finished pictures.

But even I realized the curious mixture of good and bad in the already famous collection. In certain rooms, especially in what he called his *salon*, the eighteenth century lived again, for in addition to these drawings, he had the most splendid Beauvais tapestries I had ever seen. But unfortunately he had become completely obsessed with Japanese art, and I think he was often taken in by dealers, especially with regard to Oriental china.

The most agreeable room in his house was his study, lined with both old and modern books. There were also, there, a few exquisite pastels. All over the house were water-colours painted by his brother Jules. I do not think they have ever been shown. They are very fine, and recall the work of the early English water-colourists. When I expressed admiration of these paintings, I did not know they were the work of his brother. What I said delighted him, but I felt he had no idea of their beauty. He liked them because they recalled his adored Jules. Jules' water-colours showed he was a real artist, and in no sense an amateur. But for his brother, I believe he would have been a painter and not a writer, for during tours he made in North Africa and later in Italy he seemed to have spent all his time painting. Edmond also painted, and I recall a water-colour portrait of his brother which I could not help feeling probably gave a truer picture of that unhappy, gifted being than did any of the many busts and portraits done by well-known sculptors and artists. To that I make an exception for the celebrated lithograph done by Gavarni (in 1853) showing the two brothers sitting on a small couch side by side.

I spent the whole of that afternoon with Edmond de Goncourt, and he told me many facts concerning his early life with Jules, and of the books they had written together. To me those hours opened a window on to a France I had not known existed, full of enchantment to the eager girl I then was.

But on my return to London, my troubles began. Mr. Heinemann thought there ought to be two volumes, and as I knew that though I had a generous publisher, I could not hope to make much money out of such a translation as that I had planned, I decided I had better ask some one to write the book with me. The lady I selected was Miss Marie Shedlock, who later made a great reputation in America as a lecturer, and teller of stories in children's schools.

Neither of us had any idea how such a collaboration ought to be arranged. However, we did the best we could. I did not wholly approve of her work, and she did not approve of mine. Still, this did not affect our friendship. The two volumes duly appeared. They were beautifully produced, and there were eight fine illustrations, but the edition must have been a small one, for the book seldom appears in a second-hand catalogue. It was widely reviewed; there was evidently, however, a general feeling, summed up in the first sentence of a long notice in *The Guardian*: "It is not easy to understand what object the compilers of this book about the brothers de Goncourt had before them." An English acquaintance told Monsieur de Goncourt that the translation had brought in a very large sum, so when he asked me how much I had made, and was told a thousand francs (£40), he was much puzzled.

I nearly always went to Auteuil when I was in Paris, and I enjoyed my talks with him, for he had a great knowledge of *les petits côtés de l'histoire* of a kind which was, and is, especially interesting to me. I longed to be allowed to join the party of friends he used to gather together in his attic every Sunday evening; but in time I learnt that Madame Daudet was the only woman ever asked. As I grew to know him better, Monsieur de Goncourt talked freely to me of his fellow writers. Of them all, he only cared for Daudet. As to the others, he sometimes spoke of them with contempt, and always with malice. Edmond de Goncourt was the only snobbish Frenchman I have ever known. He never forgot, I am tempted to say for a single moment, that he was *un gentilhomme Lorrain*. But it should be added he was a survival of the seventeenth, rather than the eighteenth, century. I always felt, when I was with him, that he had stepped out of a page of Saint Simon's memoirs.

There must have been a very peculiar side to the two brothers. To give an example of what I mean, they wrote their creative work with goose-quill pens, and their historical and critical work with gold pens. The manuscripts of their novels were carefully kept, and beautifully bound. Any other manuscript, the moment the book was in print, was instantly burnt. Edmond regretted this curious habit when he discovered the mad King of

Bavaria had paid a large sum for the manuscript of *La Faustin*. This study of a famous actress had appeared serially in a newspaper, and the "copy" had not been returned to the author.

·XIII

ALL those who have been interested and concerned with contemporary literature, find among the greatest changes coming their way those affecting literary reputations; and nothing that has happened in my time has so impressed me with a sense of the irony of life. Writers regarded as geniuses when I was a child, ay, and long after my childhood, are now not only forgotten, their names evoke nothing in the minds of those who regard themselves as well-read. On the other hand, writers then thought of small account are, for the present at any rate, firmly established.

The most striking example I myself have come across of this fact concerns Paul Verlaine. During the late 'eighties and quite early 'nineties, when I was a great deal in Paris, I do not recall his name having ever been mentioned to me excepting during a talk I had with Jules Lemaître, and now and again when I, myself, spoke of him. In those days, Maupassant and Loti were in a class by themselves; Zola and Daudet dominated the Paris literary scene, Bourget being a strong runner-up; there was a group of poets of whom Coppée was regarded as the most distinguished. Verlaine's genius was recognized, both in France and England, by all genuine lovers of French poetry, but in so far as there was any interest in his singular personality, it was associated with a strong repugnance for his way of life. He was pious, yet supposed to be debauched, and often drunk; in a distinguished volume of essays published a short time ago, is an echo of the feeling he then evoked, for the writer describes him as spending his life between the brothel and the confessional. Yet, whenever I

now refer to the French writers I then knew, Verlaine is the
name which seems to leap to the mind of those who care for the
French literature of the late nineteenth century. But I am always
asked how I came to know him.

The first person who spoke to me of Verlaine's verse was my
mother. In a sense poetry was her principal intellectual interest.
During her early youth (she was born in 1829), when Shelley
was still regarded as a kind of crazy anarchist, rather than as a
great poet, he became the idol of her heart. She must have been
the first to recognize the quality of Emily Brontë's verse, and
an enthusiastic reference to *Wuthering Heights* in a letter to her
then closest friend, is the only allusion to that writer I have found
in any published letter, diary, or memoir, written during the
forty years that followed.

Recalling my mother's admiration for his work, I must have
written to Verlaine at the time I was contributing a column called
"Paris Notes" to some weekly paper. They were mostly com-
posed of paragraphs concerning French creative writers. Of the
Paris society of that day, and such subjects as racing, and the
French world of sport, I knew nothing.

I remember my first meeting with Verlaine. It was in, or rather
outside, a café, in what was to me an unknown quarter of Paris.
He made a curious impression on me because he was so simple,
so gentle, so unlike the generally brilliant, malicious and, as in
the case of Zola, often self-obsessed, and almost always cynical,
writers, with whom I was then constantly in contact. We became
at once on kindly, friendly terms, and after this meeting, whenever I went to Paris, I would send him one of the *petits bleus*
which reached the person addressed far quicker than a telegram.
Sometimes there came no answer. But when he made an appointment to see me, it was always at one of two cafés, and I would
go off to spend an hour with *le pauvre Lélian,* as some one called
him. I never saw him I will not say drunk, but even in any way

muddled or muzzy. He was always treated with marked respect by the waiters, as well as by the other frequenters of the café where we had what was usually an hour's talk.

When with me he always spoke of what had happened twenty years before, and I would listen, moved, to his pitiful accounts of how happy he had been during his brief married life, and as he referred, with painful emotion, to the son he had never seen, or if he had seen him, only as an infant. He talked as if he still had a hope that some day his wife would come back to him. Yet, even then, Madame Verlaine, taking advantage of the French divorce law, had married again, as he must surely have known, though I was not aware of it.

As to their parting, he blamed himself, though far more than himself her mother and stepfather. Those two people were the only human beings of whom I ever heard Verlaine speak with the kind of passion of hate Frenchmen feel for those they despise, or feel have done them an injury. *La Bonne Chanson*, which contains some of the most exquisite love lyrics written, I think it may be said in any language, was addressed to his wife.

To me he never uttered Rimbaud's name, but I gradually became aware that those of his fellow writers who saw him from time to time, ascribed all his misfortunes to the fellow genuis who wrote *Le Bateau ivre*. Not that any of them at that time would have admitted Rimbaud had genius. All would have followed Jacques Blanche in describing him as *un mauvais petit drôle*.

Now and again, but far less often than of his wife and son, Verlaine would talk to me of his mother, for whose memory he seemed to cherish a great devotion—as he was indeed right to do, for she must have been one of the most understanding of mothers of sons who ever lived. On one occasion, when I got up and said "*Maman m'attend*," he gave a kind of cry, "*Maman?* That is what I always called my mother!"

Verlaine never struck me as having anything about him of the natural bohemian, and all those who are sufficiently interested in the man to have taken the trouble to know something of his life, apart from his disastrous friendship with Rimbaud, are aware he came from the dullest, narrowest, most conventional stratum of French society, the *petite bourgeoisie*, that is, the real middle class. During many years of his early life he had been a humble civil servant, and he once actually told me he might possibly be one again, as he had been "faithful and diligent," should he become, as he apparently still thought possible, reconciled to his wife!

I have known seven men I regarded as possessing genius. All seven were simple in manner, and seemed unaware, or at any rate in no way vain, of their divine gift. Of the seven, Verlaine was the simplest and the most modest. I am aware that to assert all geniuses are simple and modest would be absurd, especially when one recalls Donne, Swift, Byron, and Browning. But of the many men I have known in the last sixty years who were each acclaimed as a genius in their day, and who certainly thought themselves so, I cannot recall even one who was simple in manner, and honestly modest concerning his work.

The British near-genius is far more *naïf* than is his French brother. A clever Frenchman, and all near-geniuses are clever, is always uneasily aware that there are people about who question his right to the position he has won. But such a suspicion does not seem to cross the mind of his British opposite number.

To return to Verlaine. I cannot recall who was the moving spirit among the group of English writers who decided to send him an invitation to come to England. Whoever it was did a kind and generous action, and gave him what he felt to be the kind of recognition he had never received in a foreign country. Now and again he wandered off to Belgium, and once even to Holland, to earn a little money by giving a series of the *conférences*, or lectures, which were then the fashion. But he had never been welcomed—*choyé* was the word he used—as he was in England.

The first person who spoke to me of his coming visit was Mr. William Heinemann, and that because he knew I regarded myself as French. During his stay here I wrote about him in the papers to which I then contributed, though no editor would allow him to be described as a great French poet. Indeed I recall my anger at a reference to some splendid passage in *Sagesse* being deleted.

Certain of his kind hosts and admirers were, I suspected at the time, disappointed at finding him so different a man from what some of his verse might have led them to expect him to be. But they all worked manfully on his behalf, and he was introduced to many well-known people. To my sorrow I was not asked to join in what would have given me delight, the visit of Verlaine to George Meredith. I remember feeling secretly convinced, as I, also, had had the good fortune to be taken to see Mr. Meredith, that the two men would have nothing in common. Although Meredith had written a magnificent poem in honour of France, I should have been surprised to learn that before their meeting he had read a line of Verlaine. But I have no doubt that the then famous writer, who was a prince of courtesy, had made himself acquainted with certain of the Frenchman's poems. All the same, Meredith, who was fastidious, must have looked with distaste at one who gave the impression, as one of those who entertained him said, privately, to me, of "a poor old vagabond whose way of life was marked only too clearly on his face."

Verlaine was sensitively aware of his extreme ugliness, and he felt vexed when the foremost English caricaturist of that day made a brilliant sketch of him. I think it was a commission from William Heinemann, and for a time it was given a place of honour in that gentleman's study.

There occurred one *contretemps* which caused both anger and dismay. The heads of certain Oxford colleges were shocked at the suggestion that Verlaine should pollute the Oxford air. But in the end they were placated, and he gave a *conférence* there, but in what, as I wrote to my mother, I feared had been a hole-and-corner way.

I think Verlaine at times felt lonely and lost in London, even when surrounded by those who felt for him an enthusiastic admiration. I used to feel touched by the way he clung to me, always asking me eagerly, each time we parted, when we were to meet again. I used to see him in some pleasant chambers in the Temple, lent to him by that kindest of men, and delicately perfect writer, Arthur Symons.

Ever since those far-away days, I have never passed by, or through, Fountain Court, without returning in thought to a late morning spent with Verlaine in Symons' sitting-room. He seemed very unhappy, and went back with bitter melancholy to twenty-odd years before, and the wretched life he had then led in London. He said, "It was then I endured my Purgatory. No doubt I had often sinned, but I was compelled to undergo ferocious punishment, even before I repented of my sins." And, as he always did when with me, he dwelt on his longing to obtain his wife's forgiveness. Then, suddenly he stopped speaking. The bells of one of the city churches had begun striking twelve. Verlaine's face cleared, and he suggested we should say the Angelus. So this we did, kneeling side by side.

I have often been with a fellow Catholic when twelve o'clock began striking, but that was the first and last time such a suggestion was ever made to me.

What struck him most when he made this third visit to London, was the difference in the lighting of the streets. He had always had trouble with his eyes, and was extremely short-sighted. He remembered London (as some of his verses show only too well) as a place not only of misery and poverty, but of darkness; so during his visit in the 'nineties, he was greatly impressed by what he called the illumination of the town.

He was not only much pleased, he was also much astonished, by the enthusiasm and the kindness with which he was received, and he consulted me with regard to what he should say in an article he had been asked to write for some French paper concerning his impressions of London. I felt flattered, but naturally nervous, as to what I should advise. He wrote one sentence which touched and amused me, for it ran: *"Définitivement je suis un poète. Je n'en suis ni plus riche, ni plus fier pour ça."* And indeed both these assertions were true.

He and I once had a long talk on Hell and the Devil. Both Hell itself, and the Devil as an entity, were to him intensely real. Indeed he spoke as if Hell is a city much like Paris, and he told me he had a vivid image in his mind of what the Devil looks like. He believed in the existence of a great number of minor devils, and to them he put down many of the terrible things which happen to human beings in this world. He also believed the Devil occasionally takes the form of a man; and he wrote two singular poems on that theme. One tells how a woman falls passionately in love, her lover being, as a matter of fact, the Devil. Gradually she comes to suspect the truth, without her love being at all affected. Indeed there comes a time when she says, "I know you for what you are; and I intend to be damned, for thus alone can I ensure we shall never be parted." But the Devil, in that like many human members of his sex, has by now wearied of the poor soul, and disappears. However, he has not done with her, for she kills herself, and so having committed a mortal sin, finds herself in Hell.

He himself preferred the verses in which he tells the story of a woman who, with her lover, murders her husband by cutting off his head. Suddenly the lips of the dead man open, and he exclaims, "I was in a state of mortal sin when you killed me! But I still love you, and as you have committed murder you will be damned, and so we shall be in Hell, and eternally together." But the wife repenting, calls on God to pity her. So when she dies, she goes to Heaven.

Verlaine had a most attaching voice. It was a very gentle voice, and he pronounced his words in an exquisite way. I agreed with Lemaître who observed, "Every sentence he utters sounds like a caress." That same delightful man and fine writer also declared what indeed was true, "Verlaine is the only one of us who had no master." Lemaître much envied Verlaine his simple faith, and the last time I saw him, he said with the queer ironic smile which often played on his kind face, "I wish I had sinned as he has sinned, so as to be able, like him, to repent."

Sagesse undoubtedly played a certain part in the religious revival which occurred in France during and after the last war. Yet when, years after it had been published, Maurice Barrès wished to procure a copy, he had difficulty in finding one. Incidentally, by far the finest of the many eulogies written immediately after Verlaine's death was by Barrès.

As the years went on, largely owing to Barrès, the younger men all came to know and honour Verlaine, and one great joy and glory came to him. This was his election as *Maître des Poètes*. What naturally delighted him was that this title is bestowed on a poet by his fellow poets, and on this occasion, the election honoured the electors more than the elected. It certainly would have pleased him, and I hope he knew, even if he was then in Purgatory, that his successor was Mallarmé.

The last time I saw him, he described to me at great length a terrible illness he had had during his married life, when his young wife nursed him devotedly. He had this illness in mind when he wrote some verses he called *"A ma Femme."*

I should like to note one curious fact. This is that every portrait of Verlaine I have ever seen recalls him vividly, though by far the best is a drawing by Sir William Rothenstein which was, I think, drawn during his last visit to London.

All I know of his son is that he sent out his father's *faire-part*, though I heard he did not "conduct the mourning" at Verlaine's funeral.

XIV

AT the time I first met Alphonse Daudet he was about fifty, and I repeat what was certainly true—he and Zola dominated the French literary scene, though Daudet, unlike Zola, shrank from any form of self-advertisement.

Of the many French and English writers I have known well, Daudet remains in my memory as having possessed the most remarkable personality. He seemed to me to be far greater as a man, than as the author of his then famous novels. All the same, I am surprised his place as historian of the Second Empire, and of the France of the 'seventies and 'eighties of the last century, is not recognized as, in my opinion, it should be. Owing to his having been the personal secretary and intimate younger friend of the Duc de Morny, he had a knowledge of the Court of the Tuilleries, and of the political and social worlds of that day, no French writer I have known, or whose memoirs or letters I have read, could touch. *Les Rois en exil, Le Nabab, Numa Roumestan*, each contains a fine gallery of portraits; and the painter of those men and women had no prejudices, and no preferences, to deflect his vision. He drew straight from life as he remembered it.

My French grandmother had a sixth sense, which I have inherited from her, which tells the reader of the coming of a writer who will, in time, take a great place among his fellows. I do not mean, by that, popularity. The first novel written by Daudet at once impressed Madame Swanton Belloc as possessing a quality lacking in any of the younger creative artists of that somewhat arid time. She and my mother, as the years went on, read everything that Daudet wrote, and *Fromont jeune et Risler aîné* was soon put into my hands. It is a remarkable book, worthy to be on the same shelf as the German *Debit and Credit*. In that curiously different from Daudet's other books, *Fromont jeune et Risler aîné* owed little or nothing to his own experience of life.

We became friends from the first hour I spent with him in his plainly furnished study. The Daudets' apartment was in the rue de Bellechasse, on the left bank of the Seine, and consisted of a few large rooms. He could not get up to greet a visitor, for he suffered from an acute form of arthritis, and was always in pain. The strongly marked features of his pale face were surmounted by a shock of grey-black hair, and his body had become the wreck of a powerfully built man. He had a simple, kindly manner, and was an amazingly brilliant and varied talker. I never heard him even allude in his every day life, to any of his books. He was passionately interested in every sort of human creature, and was always willing to see, advise, and encourage any young person who wished to write.

I doubt if any man was ever kinder and more selfless with regard to those of his own craft than was Alphonse Daudet. He was the only literary man or woman I have ever known who went on reading manuscripts sent him by unknown people, and telling them what he thought of their work. He remembered his own beginnings, and how two French writers of the day had sent him back the manuscript of his first novel, saying they had had to make it a rule to refuse to look at any work submitted to them for an opinion. And were that the only thing to Daudet's credit, I think it proves him to have been, as was once said to me by Ebner, his devoted friend and secretary, a man of inexhaustible kindness of heart.

I was recently astonished, amused, and disgusted, to read in a long biography of Émile Zola, an allusion to Alphonse Daudet's "extra-marital relations." One could not be with either of them for even a very short time, without realizing how absorbed in each other were Julia and Alphonse Daudet. Though, in that unlike his wife, he enjoyed being surrounded by his kind, they lived, both when in Paris and in the country, what used to be called a *pot-au-feu* existence, and were never apart. They had only been married ten years, he being still under forty at the time, when he was struck down with a crippling form of rheumatism. So if instead of loving his wife with all his heart, as he most certainly did, he had hated her, it would have been impossible for him to have started what Zola's biographer delicately called "extra-marital relations." It was Julia who made of him the writer he became. Lemaître said of the Daudets that, had they not married, Alphonse would have frittered away his life, leaving but a pencilled signature on the noble pages of the history of French literature.

When, after having grown to know them both well, I was about to write an account of him for an American magazine, he begged me earnestly to say he and his wife collaborated in the closest way when he was writing a novel; and he added he always took her advice as to whether a certain passage should be altered, or even deleted. But great as was her influence over him, she had soon given up trying to make him write each day at a certain time, as she would have liked him to do. After idling for many weeks, he would suddenly begin a new book, writing for twelve hours out of the twenty-four for as long as a month, and not even breaking off to have the midday meal which has always played a considerable part in the day-to-day French life. Julia believed the breakdown in his health was partly owing to what had been his methods of work during the first ten years of their married life. She was twenty, Alphonse seven years older, at the time of their marriage, and for some time they had been so poor that, unknown to him, she frequently put her humble jewels in pawn. When I knew him, he had the same kind of bitter horror of poverty which Bernard Shaw, who possesses certain of Daudet's fine human qualities of kindness and compassion, once expressed.

In a talk with Daudet concerning his youth, and this was the only time he ever spoke to me at length of himself, he told me he ascribed his arthritis to the fact that for three years he and his brother Ernest had lived, if living it could be called, on under a hundred francs a month. They came from a family of seventeen children, and had left the south of France to make their fortune, as they thought, in Paris, the one being then seventeen, and the other nineteen.

When I first knew Madame Daudet she was a little over forty, and quite unlike any Frenchwoman I had ever known. She had a prim reserved manner, and evidently prided herself, with every right to do so, on her housewifely qualities. Yet the façade of *une bonne bourgeoise* concealed, as I came gradually to know, a woman of great intelligence, and of strong determination of character. In those days she seemed to me very silent but, when she spoke, it was with what I felt to be absolute frankness.

I once went to see them when there had been what was then called an *esclandre*, between a young dramatic author and his wife. He had fallen in love with an actress playing the leading rôle in one of his plays and, filled with jealous rage, the wife had gone back to her parents. With more emotion than I had ever seen her show, or was ever to see her show, Julia told me that when Alphonse had made his first success on the stage, some cruel friend had told her he was certain to fall in love with one of his interpreters, each of whom would certainly do her best to attract him. And then she added, in a way which moved me at the time, that she never allowed him to guess how frightened she felt, as she looked at herself in the glass, and saw how little she could hope to compete with the beautiful and clever women with whom he was constantly thrown, when rehearsing his play. "Alphonse, who thinks he knows so much of men and women, never guessed the agonies I used to go through, if he came back an hour, or say two hours, later than he had said he would do." She exclaimed, with deep feeling, how terrible it must be for a devoted wife to feel a husband's love slipping away; but added, with the shrewd good sense which was, I think, her leading quality, "Unless a woman intends to break for ever with the father of her children, she ought at any rate to pretend she knows nothing of his change of heart."

This talk made a deep impression on me, and I wrote an account of it to my mother, the same evening.

Had I not thought well of her for other reasons, I should have admired Madame Daudet wholeheartedly for the kindly way she endured the constant presence, both in Paris, and in her country home, of cranky, touchy Edmond de Goncourt. I used to wonder why and how he had become the Daudets' *ami de la maison.*

When I was a young woman, almost every well-to-do French family we knew had a friend, sometimes a lonely woman, oftener a bachelor, who was with them constantly. He came, for instance, to dinner every Sunday in Paris, and always stayed with them in the country each summer. But the position of de Goncourt in the Daudet household was far more than that. They were his only intimates, indeed it may be said his only friends, for he was not liked, and he did nothing to make himself liked, by most of his acquaintances. The real explanation was, I fancy, as follows. Daudet had met Edmond de Goncourt soon after the death of his brother Jules, at a time when he was extremely unhappy. This alone would have aroused deep sympathy and concern in the new friend; and the older man, on his side, was naturally attracted by a writer so utterly unlike himself, and who had so agreeable a personality.

Daudet soon became the star performer at the gatherings which took place each week in what de Goncourt called his attic, and the host had sufficient knowledge of human nature to realize how exceptionally close was the tie between the husband and wife. This was why Julia Daudet became the only woman ever asked to the attic. To be so honoured naturally pleased the then young Madame Daudet, and opened, at any rate a little way, the door to her heart. Long after the birth of her two sons, a daughter was born to the Daudets; the child was named Edmée, and de Goncourt was her godfather.

But when appeared the first volume of the famous diaries, Julia became extremely disturbed. She told their now dear friend she trusted he would never put on record anything Alphonse had said, without asking if Alphonse was willing he should do so. To her indignation, he refused to give this assurance. All the same, I am sure he remembered what she had asked him to do for, with regard to Daudet, the diarist was discreet in a way he was with regard to no one else.

Léon once said to me that he and his mother accepted Edmond de Goncourt as a sort of devoted step-grandfather. But he admitted that they both felt far more at ease when their devoted step-grandfather was not there. Unfortunately for them, he was constantly there. Alone of them all, Alphonse Daudet was genuinely attached to this constant guest, and he enjoyed de Goncourt's astringent conversation. During the last years of his life, the old man spent every summer at Champsrosay, and it was there he died. If nothing else is worthy to survive of Daudet's work, his account of Edmond de Goncourt's last days and death is surely entitled to do so.

Champsrosay was half a farmhouse and half a château, and there Daudet, when I knew him, was happiest. I had the good fortune to be sometimes asked for a whole day. Arriving early, I would stay late. It was then we would have long intimate talks. Daudet was very frank, and I felt him to be free from the sort of bitterness which is characteristic of many thoughtful Frenchmen who are also writers.

He had been, as a young man, a strong advocate of the divorce law passed in 1880. But when I knew him, his views had changed, for he then thought of divorce entirely and only as affecting the children of a divorced couple. When discussing the question he once said, "Surely a child forms an unbreakable chain linking a man and a woman?" And he wrote, later, in a letter to me, "When choosing a woman to be his wife, a man must be able to say to himself, 'When I am dying these are the arms which will hold me, and hers is the hand whose fingers will close my eyes.'"

In that unlike every other Frenchman I have ever known, Daudet had a genuine horror of what used to be called free love. He told me that even a long *collage* was at best a parody of marriage. The first time he ever spoke to me of the subject I was secretly astonished to hear his vigorous condemnation of a kind of life which even then I knew was almost universally led by unmarried Parisians of every kind and condition. As logically followed, and like most Frenchmen Daudet was logical, he was an advocate of quite early marriage, and he much disapproved of the part the dowry plays in the French matrimonial system.

He only once spoke to me of the Franco-Prussian War, and surprised me by saying that his months as a private during that war remained more vividly in his mind than any other period of his existence. This was to me the stranger because he seemed to have spent those months, as did my own first cousins, in a regiment stationed in the suburbs of Paris. He said his war experiences had been too poignant to be used in any of his books. He took part in three *sorties* and, according to him, each second in each *sortie* still stood out in his memory as full of horror and excitement, as also of a kind of fierce joy.

The most terrible day of his life was the thirty-first of October, 1870. That morning information of the surrender of Metz reached Paris and, as he was known to be a good walker, he was detailed to take the news to certain of the forts round the city.

In each case he saw the Commander of the fort, and always the Commander stood in the middle of his men. While handing the letter entrusted to him, he made a point of saying, as quietly as he could force himself to do, "Bazaine is a traitor; he has betrayed his country." He said the effect on those who heard of the capitulation was far more painful than anything he had ever seen happen. "Though it be forgotten now," he observed, "in those days Bazaine had been regarded as a hero; one of the few soldiers in whom the Emperor was known to feel confidence." And it is true that to this day there are many Frenchmen to whom Bazaine's action remains as inexplicable as will be that of Pétain's surrender in time to come.

I once tried to find out Daudet's political views, for ever since my intimacy with the Déroulèdes I had felt interested in French politics. He spoke with angry contempt of the then Republican leaders, and admitted he had only three times troubled to register a vote.

Though he could not read English, and when I first knew him had never been to England, he had a considerable knowledge of English art and literature. His favourite painter of all painters was Hogarth, his favourite writer Swift. He was superstitious, and from childhood he avoided taking a journey on a Friday. He also believed in lucky and unlucky numbers. He shared a belief I have long held: that life is a balanced ration; yet he is the only man who ever said to me, "I am an absolutely happy man."

Although he always had "a good press," both during his lifetime and after his death, Daudet's material good fortune—he and Zola were said to have a working income of three hundred thousand francs a year (£12,000)—caused him to be much envied. I used occasionally to be asked why I had become so fond of him. I could have answered because he was fond of me; and also because he encouraged me to become a novelist at a time when my mother's literary friends and acquaintances all

begged me not to add to what seemed to them the flood of unwanted new books. He alone said to me what I have since often
said to would-be writers, "Of course write a novel, ay, and more
than one novel, if you feel the urge to do so! If there is any value
in your work, you will end by finding a publisher and, in time, a
public."

Some years after I had first known the Daudets, they came to
London for, I think, three weeks, and I naturally saw a good
deal of them. To the surprise of the London of 1895, they were
accompanied by their three children. Madame Daudet was distressed the little daughter was never included in the invitations
showered on them; and as they had brought no maid, Edmée
began by remaining alone, sometimes for hours, in the sitting-room
of their hotel. But, after a while, acting on the advice of her husband, Madame Daudet simply brought the child with her wherever she went, and she refused all invitations sent her by those
she thought would not welcome the little girl.

The husband and wife were impressed by the contrast, much
more apparent then than now, between the well-to-do and the
poor of London. Daudet spoke to me several times of his distress
at such scenes as were those then to be found in Hyde Park; that
is the wealth, beauty, and appearance of comfort in the "carriage
folk," while within a few yards of them lay on the grass gaunt-
looking men, women, and children, clad in rags. Some philanthropist had the unfortunate idea of taking the French writer
over a workhouse, an experience which filled him with horror.
Long after that stay in London, he told me that what had struck
him most was a drive he had taken through the East End, because
of the difference between what he called *"les deux Ends."* He
had been puzzled to see in the East End women who were apparently destitute wearing what he called luxurious rags. In those
days the poor of London seldom wore anything new. There was
an enormous trade done in second-hand clothes of a kind that

would never now be seen even on the least self-respecting beggar. A shabby, dirty hat, covered with what had been the most expensive artificial flowers worn the previous season by a débutante, would be perched on the grey hair of a charwoman; and a little girl would appear at Sunday school, in sweltering weather, in a threadbare velvet frock which had formed part, years before, of an old lady's smart evening gown.

I also had a real liking for Léon Daudet, and I followed his ill-fated life with close and painful interest. I grieve he should have died in the middle of a world war he had always foretold would come to pass.

As a youth—he was just my age—Léon was a caricature of his father; and even in a home where he was evidently exceedingly happy, and with parents he dearly loved, he often betrayed an extraordinary violence of nature. Rather later, after he had begun studying medicine against his father's advice, he wrote a novel of which the very title, *Les Morticoles,* was a challenge and insult to the whole French medical profession. The book naturally cost Julia and Alphonse Daudet many friends. But the son had none of his father's creative gift, and in time he gave up fiction, to devote himself to writing pictures of contemporary life, and especially of contemporary politics.

Léon Daudet was the only Frenchman of his generation with whom I ever came in contact, who had a lively and constant interest in English literature. I recently found a long letter from him in which he earnestly begged me to translate into French Meredith's *Egoist!* Even when I first knew him, he had a far better knowledge of Shakespeare than I had. Among his early novels was *Le Voyage de Shakespeare,* the imaginary voyage being to Denmark. He believed, and was proud of so believing, the Daudets to be descended from one of the Moors who settled in Provence; and he was overjoyed when he heard that the Moorish name David is pronounced *Dodet.* His mother liked to think that Daudet came from *Deo datus*, "Given to God."

Léon Daudet was still very young when he became engaged to Jeanne Hugo, the old poet's beloved granddaughter. Just before the wedding, Hugo declared no priest should stand between the bride and God; so, to the dismay of Julia Daudet, the ceremony was celebrated in the open air, without benefit of clergy. Jeanne was beautiful, but she had a hasty temper, and not long after their son was born, when Léon brought her the first chapter of a novel, she exclaimed, "There are already too many inkpots in our family!" and taking up an inkpot, she threw it in his face. There soon followed a divorce; but as their wedding had not been celebrated in a church, it was not a sacramental marriage, so Léon was free to marry a charming young niece of his mother's, who had always loved him. They were as happy a couple as had been Julia and Alphonse, and in his books Léon paid his wife many warm tributes.

While his brother was devoted to the Empress Eugenie, Léon, as all the world now knows, became a passionate Royalist. Given his nature, he was bound to be always "agin the government," and he was soon a festering thorn in the body of the Republican régime; this being especially true when he joined forces with the formidable Maurras.

No one, outside his own circle, could have felt more sympathy and sorrow than I felt when came the tragedy, at once so mysterious and so horrible in all its details, of the death of Léon's son, Philippe.

I have read everything written concerning the affair, and I am inclined to believe the boy (who though only fourteen looked three or four years older) was killed by the police, who, knowing nothing of his parentage, thought they had caught a dangerous young anarchist. If this theory, which was not held by any member of the Daudet family, is correct, it would account for everything that took place after the disappearance of the child. Also for the determined, successful efforts made, both by the Paris Prefect of Police, and by the then French Government, to stop the inquiry which was demanded by the public, as well as by the unfortunate parents, and which might have brought the truth to light.

Léon and his wife believed their Philippe had been deliberately done to death as an act of revenge for certain acts and writings of his father. This I find it almost, I will not say quite, impossible to credit. I feel this the more as, after all, it would have served the purpose of his enemies so much better to have murdered Daudet himself.

XV

WHEN I first came in contact with Anatole France, I was warned that he would never receive any stranger, with however good an introduction, except on the one day of the week—I think it was a Thursday—which he put aside for receiving both the known and unknown men and women who wished, as the phrase then went, to pay him their homage. I have no remembrance of the first time I went to see him. I was probably taken by some kindly friend who already knew him. But he must have asked me to return, for I saw him fairly often during the years that followed.

He lived a long way from the centre of Paris; all the same I was always surprised to see how few people cared to journey to the Villa Said, for at no time did the comparatively small study on the first floor of his house, where he held this peculiar weekly reception, seem crowded. There were naturally more men than women, and his callers belonged to every class and condition. Even schoolboys came in their black *lycée* overalls to gaze at the Master. Some of his admirers would walk backward to the door, so as to see him up to the last second of their visit. When I grew to know him really well, he confided to me that he found the foreigners most trying, as they arrived early, and stayed late. His ideal visitor was the young man, preferably a writer, who walked in, bowed deeply, pressed his hand murmuring *"Cher Maître,"* and then left.

His old housekeeper, who was by way of being a character, and of whom he was to a certain extent afraid, disliked these

gatherings, and her manner to the visitors was cold, and sometimes rude. However, she soon made a friend of me, and she
would always stop me on my way out, to tell me how truly good-
hearted, while how foolish and easily taken in, was her master.
No doubt because of my youth she never mentioned what must
have been an odious trial to her—his unedifying fugitive love
affairs.

He generally wore what seemed to me a very peculiar costume,
for it looked like a black dressing-gown. As was the case with
almost all Parisians of his generation, he had a great fear of cold,
and his fine Socratic head was almost always covered by a skull-
cap. Although I am sure he did not try to do so, he certainly
"looked the part," and had I not known he was a writer, I should
have thought him a famous painter.

At last came the day when he asked me to call on him one
morning when he was to be alone. I think Mr. Harry Cust, then
editing the *Pall Mall Gazette,* may have asked me to write something about him. We settled down to a real talk, and I told him
that of his books I preferred, by far, what is still the comparatively little known *Histoire Comique.* I recently re-read that
wonderful picture of sophisticated human nature, and I felt
filled with the same admiration I had felt when first reading the
book fifty years ago.

No work of imagination known to me in French or English
gives so true and agonizing a picture of jealousy, a passion so
rarely treated in fiction, partly perhaps because only those who
are at the moment experiencing that torturing passion seem
able to feel any sympathy with its victims. Jealousy, in the great
majority of cases, arouses cruel amusement, rather than understanding sympathy. When I make this claim for *Histoire Comique*
I do not forget the other great French picture of the passion drawn
by Proust.

Anatole France confirmed what I had felt certain was the

case when I read the book; every character in *Histoire Comique* was taken straight from life.

Next to *Histoire Comique* I preferred *Thaïs*. France told me that *Thaïs* was the outcome of a passage read by him in a small volume, published in the seventeenth century, which contained short lives of the Monks of the Desert. In a dry, colourless little paragraph he found the kernel of his romance. Before beginning the book, he made a prolonged and close study of a period of religious history of which up to then he had known nothing. He also procured maps of North Africa published in every country, and he had plans drawn of the country round Alexandria. I thought it strange he had not taken the trouble to go there himself; but evidently the thought of taking such a journey had never occurred to him. He had a queer kind of liking for *Le Lys rouge,* which is, to me, his one poor novel. Perhaps a reason why I disliked *Le Lys rouge* was because it contains caricatures of two people I knew. The one was Verlaine, and the other Violet Paget, who wrote under the name of Vernon Lee. I doubt if Anatole France had ever met Verlaine; but I am sure he knew Miss Paget. She lived in Florence; but she was often in England; and I came to know her fairly well. She was one of the few writers known to me with whom I felt no sympathy; this partly because she was extremely erudite, which frightened me, and also extremely snobbish, which made me feel ill-at-ease in her company.

When it is remembered Anatole France often attempted to reconstitute the past, it may be of interest to recall his theory, as expounded to me, that all a novelist can hope to achieve is what he called a vision, or poetic *aperçue,* wholly personal to the writer. This was to me the stranger as he denied, with more violence than he generally showed, that human nature changes with time. He felt contempt for what he called the so-called realists, and declared nothing any one of them had written could compare, as to sharply etched realism, with the then lately discovered *Mimes of Herondas.*

On another occasion, when we were alone, he suddenly talked to me of his daughter. He had a small portrait of her painted by Boutet de Monval, and it was that of a pretty little girl who recalled in no way her father. His housekeeper told me Anatole France always moved this picture about with him from room to room.

At that time I was seeing a good deal of the Daudets, and I was astonished to find that whereas Daudet held the widest, most liberal, views, as to the freedom which should be allowed by parents to their daughters, as well as to their sons, in the matter of marriage, Anatole France evidently believed in the strait-laced French bourgeois liking for a carefully arranged marriage. He was no doubt unconsciously influenced by what his mother would have felt as to the upbringing and settlement in life of the daughter she had longed for, and never had. France's ideal of womanhood was his mother, and he told me once, in a dry unemotional tone, that as he grew older, she was perpetually in his thoughts. He never mentioned his wife, and I felt it impossible to visualize him as having led the life of the average French middle-class husband. Yet that he had led that narrow respectable form of existence was proved, to me, by something told me by a fellow writer who knew him well.

The only man of whom I ever heard Anatole France speak with warm affection was Renan. At a time when he was young and quite unknown, Renan had encouraged him, and told him to persevere, saying, "Always aim to achieve the best that is in you." It was Renan who suggested to him *Le Procurateur de Judée.* He and Renan were talking together, and Renan declared that the things described in the Gospels must have made a deep impression on those who took part in them. This France denied, and Renan, smiling, said something tantamount to "Then, in your view, Pontius Pilate, in old age . . ."

France once told me journalism should prove an excellent apprenticeship for any man or woman who wished to do creative work, and he pointed out that Pascal's famous Letters were, after all, journalism.

I am sorry I never met Madame de Caillavet. But I feel certain she did not play as great a part in his literary life and work as was claimed by her friends. She, and they, were fond of representing him as extremely lazy and the kind of writer who has to be constantly prodded. What makes me feel certain this was not true was that whenever I spent an hour with him, his mind was obviously dwelling on his creative work, and he spoke to me who, after all, did not see him very often, of a number of novels he hoped to write, and some of which he did write, in the years that followed. One of the unwritten books was to have the splendid title of *Les Autels de la Peur*.

The one quality or trait in which Anatole France seemed to me deficient, and it is a rare deficiency in a Frenchman who either writes or paints, was humour. He was extremely angry when some spiteful friend told him that a wit had observed that whereas Lemaître was Renan's spiritual adviser, he, France, was Renan's monkey, whose *singeries* (surely an untranslatable word) were kept for the philosopher's lighter hours. He had no liking for Lemaître, this perhaps owing to the fact that this delightful and underestimated writer had at one time loved the same lady, and she had thrown France over for Lemaître.

I thought it strange he lived in a new, fashionable quarter, as he so loved the old Paris where he had been born. He told me his only idle hours were spent wandering along the quays, on that long stretch of pavement where are the boxes filled with books for sale. He claimed to have occasionally bought a really rare volume for a few sous.

I may have lost something through his always treating me as *une jeune fille*, with whom certain subjects could not be discussed.

On the other hand, my youth, both in the case of Verlaine and Anatole France, caused them unconsciously to show me a side of their minds and hearts they evidently showed to few.

He sometimes spoke with strong admiration of certain writers. He seemed to know Balzac by heart, preferring (which disappointed and surprised me) the *Contes drolatiques*. But to him Flaubert was the supreme master of French prose, and he singled out *Trois Contes* as containing Flaubert's best work.

Of the Frenchmen I have known, Anatole France was, at that time, the only out and out pacifist. Yet when came the outbreak of war in 1914, he was so horrified and so moved that he actually made a serious attempt to get into the Army. During one of those four war years he came to London. Mrs. Asquith kindly asked me to meet him in what was then the beautiful drawing-room of 10 Downing Street, and when I next saw him he spoke to me with delight of one of our hostess' eighteenth-century pictures. But at the time, though there were very few people there, and though they all spoke French, and were obviously well acquainted with his work, he seemed what I should have thought impossible, intimidated. I cannot help thinking he knew nothing of England and, apart from *The Canterbury Tales,* of which he once spoke to me with something like passionate enthusiasm, he had read none of the great British classics, with the exception of *Robinson Crusoe, A Sentimental Journey, Clarissa Harlowe,* and certain novels of Sir Walter Scott. Of these he thought supreme *The Bride of Lammermoor.*

Whenever I went to Paris I called on Zola. This for the following reason. He was convinced, I feel sure wrongly, that the more a novelist as a man, rather than as a writer, is mentioned in the papers and magazines of his own and other countries, the more his novels will be read. As to that, though in nothing else, he exactly resembled Hall Caine.

At the end of the 'eighties, and early in the 'nineties, everything Zola wrote enjoyed what now seems an extraordinary *succès de scandale,* and his name must have been known to millions of people who had never read one of his books. Thus he was always "news." From, say, 1889, till he fled to England fearing the rigours of a French prison in connection with the trial and condemnation which had followed his advocacy of Dreyfus, several editors for whom I was then writing would willingly commission an article dealing with whatever book he happened to be then writing.

He always seemed glad to see me, receiving me with a kind of melancholy courtesy and, what seemed to me flattering, recalling what we had discussed at our last meeting. I was very simple in those days, and I never told myself that, given the sort of man he was, and the views held by him, he naturally made, and kept, notes of each of our talks.

I feel sure Zola never wasted a whole minute in his life. As far as any of those about him then knew, his only form of relaxation was going to the Hôtel des Ventes with Madame Zola. Their house in Paris was filled—crammed is the right word—with large pieces of what they believed to be mediæval furniture, as well as bric-à-brac of every kind. I remember telling myself that some squares of oak panelling he had bought straight out of a château, were alone undoubtedly genuine. Yet the only time I ever saw his sad, sallow face light up into eager pleasure, was when he showed me an immense bed he believed had been the bed of Diane de Poitiers. Even as to the tapestries which hung in almost every room, and on the staircase, I had doubts, for I knew there was a factory where tapestries were being made which sometimes deceived the most competent European collectors. All the same, the sight of Zola's tapestries always gave me pleasure, for whether old or faked, they were beautiful, and that could not be said of anything else in his Paris house.

He was simple in speech, straightforward in manner, and I

never saw in him a trace of the pomposity and vanity with which he was credited. I fear he did not know himself how good was some of his work, for to him *L'Argent* was on the same level of achievement as *L'Assommoir* and *Germinal*. As to this last book, when I told him how much my mother admired *Germinal*, I was amused at his astonishment that any respectable Englishwoman should have been willing to admit she had read even one of his novels. I did not tell him she drew the line at *La Terre*, which she believed to be an innately false picture. In that view she was supported by our village doctor at La Celle Saint Cloud, who was in constant touch with the peasants, their wives, and children, in the stretch of country where are laid the scenes of *La Terre*. There was even at one time talk of a protest being signed by the country doctors of La Bauce.

The novel he most enjoyed writing was *La Bête humaine*. He had by then became acquainted with a number of railwaymen who, to his mind, were the finest-natured, and most intelligent, of those he called "the workers" of his country. He was a strong individualist, and deprecated any kind of State interference in the lives of the people. Yet he regarded it as certain that State socialism would be established in time all over the world. He told me he was glad he would be dead when that came to pass, as he valued freedom far above everything within the compass of man, and he considered any form either of enforced work, or enforced rest, to be slavery.

With the one exception of Alphonse Daudet, all Zola's fellow-writers heartily disliked him, and, in certain cases foolishly and meanly denied him any talent. All the well-known French novelists of that day had a circle of disciples and friends who admired their work, and vigorously defended them against any kind of attack. The only one of them of which this was not true was Zola. He was indeed a singularly friendless man.

Though he publicly stated on some occasion that Daudet was

his one intimate, I never met him in the Daudets' house, and Léon would often make cruel fun of him. He was so engaged one evening, while I was dining at Champsrosay, when suddenly his father exclaimed, "After you have written, my dear boy, the equivalent of one page of *L'Assommoir* or *Nana,* I will permit you to turn Zola into mockery." This was the only time I ever heard Daudet speak sharply to his son, though they often had vehement discussions, during the course of which they generally disagreed. But Léon worshipped his father, while never having the sense to take his advice. There are many allusions to Zola in the various volumes of reminiscences written in later life by Léon Daudet, but they all suffer from obvious animus. To give one instance. Léon makes a number of allusions to the way Zola mispronounced certain words. Thus, again and again he states that in place of a *j* he always used a *v,* saying for instance, *veunesse* instead of *jeunesse.* I never noticed his doing that. On an occasion when Léon observed that Zola reminded him of a London fog, his mother sharply rebuked him, as she thought my feelings would be hurt at such a comparison!

Zola was curiously imperceptive, and evidently quite unaware of the instinctive dislike with which he was regarded by many people. At the time he started his public advocacy of Dreyfus, and wrote his magnificent *J'Accuse,* he undoubtedly did Dreyfus far more harm than good in his own country.

I was never asked to Médan, though I longed to go there, because of the famous volume of short stories *Les Soirées de Médan,* which had been planned in Zola's country home. But well as I grew to know Émile Zola, I only twice spoke to his wife, and each time for only a few minutes.

In spite of what was then his great fame, and of his almost childish joy in that fame, Zola always looked ill and unhappy, the expression of his face being what the French call *tourmentée.* I now know he was going through a difficult time with Madame

Zola, for he had already formed a connection with the young woman by whom he had two children. This caused cruel amusement to certain of his fellow writers, as he had been fond of describing himself as an exceptionally faithful husband. Indeed as one of them said to me contemptuously, he seemed to have marital fidelity on the brain. So when he not only took a mistress, but chose her among the members of his household, the shock to Madame Zola was severe, and caused her bitter indignation. But she must have had a streak of great nobility in her nature, for after Zola's death, she induced his son and daughter to take his name, and she left them the large fortune which had become hers, owing to their marriage having been contracted under the *régime de la communauté.*

It should always be remembered that Zola's father and mother were Italian. Unlike the average French author, he passionately resented any criticism of his work, and would write at great length in answer to even unknown people who wrote him abusive letters.

I had many long talks with George Moore on French literature during the last three years of his life. As is well known, he strongly disliked all contemporary writers, whether French or English. Indeed, as a rule he even hated them more than he hated their books, which is indeed saying a great deal. When I was with him I used to feel glad I was not famous, as he would, in that case, have hated me, too. And of all the French writers for whom he had a lively hatred, he loathed Zola more than all the others. Yet there had been a time, as he unwillingly admitted, when the two had been friends, and I once forced him to agree that *L'Assommoir* had been a splendid achievement. Although he was sincere in all he said, I think he had never forgiven Zola for having refused to write a preface to a French translation of *A Mummer's Wife.* Zola had promised to write the preface, and then had drawn back because of some over-frank criticisms of his methods of work published by Moore in a review. But, whatever the reason, Moore spoke of him with scorn, declaring that Zola, for many years before his death, had only written for money, and thought only of money. He instanced *La Terre*, which he declared Zola must have known would attract an entirely new public—the peasants—as well as create a tremendous pother among all Frenchmen who loved France. I entirely disagreed as to his belief Zola thought only of money. Had that been true, it would have been said of him in Paris, and as far as I know, it never was. George Moore was also keenly irritated by Zola's delight in every form of advertisement. I thought this unfair, for after all, every writer wishes his work to be read, and Zola, rightly or wrongly, was convinced that the kind of publicity he encouraged, caused his books to be more widely known. Moore told me with malicious joy he had once heard Madame Zola observe that her husband had felt much disturbed on learning that some Paris *concierge* had never heard of him!

I tried to make Moore admit that Zola's advocacy of Dreyfus had been a noble action, and one which had seriously affected for a time the sale of his books. But he would not even assent to these undoubted facts. Another time, when we were talking of Zola, for he often went back to the days when he had lived in Paris, and to the men he had then known, I began to laugh. He asked suspiciously why I was laughing, and I said that if he could talk as he did of a dead Zola, I wondered what he could have found to say when Zola was enjoying his triumphant visit to England.

I saw Zola fairly often during the weeks he spent in London. He was much fêted, and I remember a public dinner which was attended by almost every British writer of distinction; he was also the guest of honour at many smaller gatherings to which I was asked, because I spoke French. Not till years later did I become aware that while in England he had taken a country house where he spent a great deal of time with his two children and their mother.

I regard his short novel *Thérèse Raquin* as his one perfect piece of creative work. But I can re-read most of his novels, and, as I re-read them, I tell myself that Balzac, on whom he modelled himself, would have had no reason to feel ashamed of his pupil.

Even when I was in London, I read all the new French books I could get hold of, and for a time I subscribed to a French circulating library. This being so, I kept up with the younger writers, and I had an intense wish to meet Barrès, whom I regarded, as did most French critics, as a far finer writer than Anatole France. But I could never persuade any of my editors that his personality would be of interest to English readers.

My mother and my brother took a lively and intelligent interest in science. My interest was lively, but not intelligent, because I knew then, and still know, nothing about science. But some one spoke to me of the great work being done by Richet, and I therefore asked the editor of *The Humanitarian* whether I might write a paper on him. The editor, a singular being named Victoria Woodhull Martin, consented, and the next time I went to Paris I wrote and asked Monsieur Richet if I might call on him.

He was at the time professor of physiology at the Paris Faculty of Medicine, as well as editor of *La Revue Scientifique*. He himself had never been a medical man, yet he was greatly in advance of his time, and especially of his French time, as regarded everything connected with health and the prevention of disease. As I at once discovered, Pasteur was his god, and he began our talk by asking me aggressively why Pasteur was not more thought of in England.

I raised the question of the wide prevalence, in France, of typhoid. Every younger member of my family had by then had this disease, excepting my brother and myself. Marcel Ballot had nearly died, and his attack of typhoid permanently affected his health. I said, but it simply amused Richet, though it was unhappily only too true, that the spread of typhoid was probably largely owing to the installation in so many French houses, and in all French hotels, of what was called *le comfort anglais*—that is water drainage, instead of the cesspool system. He admitted, however, that he had often pointed out that an apparently slight mistake made by a sanitary engineer, might bring about the death of hundreds of people from typhoid.

He spoke with bitter anger of the way in which inventors and scientists, and especially precursors, are treated by their own generation. He told me that he had invented a new word to describe the horror with which new knowledge is regarded. That word was neophobia. He said all thinking human beings are more or less neophobes, and the older men and women grow, the more neophobe they become. And he recalled with acrid satisfaction the fact that Thiers had made a speech in the 'forties, in which one sentence ran, "Do any of you seriously believe that the railway will ever take the place of the stage-coach?"

My mother had always taken an interest in spiritualism. One of her uncles by marriage, a hard-headed lawyer, must have become one of the first practising spiritualists in England. She knew Crookes, and believed him to be a scrupulously honest man; certain things he had told her as to his personal experiences of the phenomena had much impressed her. So I, too, though I then knew little, if anything, of the subject, shared my mother's interest.

I was aware Richet was credited with being a spiritualist, and I boldly asked him if this were true. The question evidently took him aback, and he was surprised I had heard of what I soon saw was at that time, on his part, a considerable concern with occurrences which, to his type of scientific mind, seemed incredible.

He told me he followed carefully the proceedings of the British Society for Psychical Research, and that he had also something to do with *Les Annales de sciences psychologiques*. But he had become convinced that to a grain of truth, there is a barrelful of fraud. Yet he told me, at great length, the story of a youthful medium, son of a butcher in Brunswick, who, at the age of two, read manuscripts in German and Latin without having learnt to read. Monsieur Richet had seen the child, and said that he appeared quite normal. Though this Frenchman did not say so, the boy must have been a typical little German, for his principal amusement was playing with tin soldiers.

Richet was obviously a man of strong convictions, and of violent feelings. He regarded Paul Déroulède with something like hatred, and called every form of militarism "this modern curse." He especially resented compulsory military service, and spoke with bitter anger of the fact that before a young Frenchman could go into a profession, or start some sort of intellectual work, he was compelled to be in the ranks for three years. He told me, with evident satisfaction, that innumerable young men took up some form of Government service simply to avoid military service. He passionately resented the fact that a youth who intended to be a doctor—and there was a shortage of doctors in France— had to serve a year as a private, and should he not pass his medical examinations by the time he was twenty-five, was compelled to complete his full term of soldiering. He thought, however, that what he described as France's state of military servitude conferred a benefit on women, as they could take the place of the young men. I was surprised to find he was what was then called a feminist. He much admired the young Russian Jewesses who came to Paris, often almost penniless, to take up medicine and science. He told me he had then working in his laboratory a Russian girl of fifteen, who had gone through all her medical examinations in six months, and who could speak not only Russian, French, and

German, but also Greek and Latin.

Charles Richet made a very great impression on me: a far greater impression than that made on me some forty years later by Sir Oliver Lodge. For one thing, he impressed me by what I felt to be an exceptionally noble outlook on life, and his desire to leave something which would be of permanent value to suffering humanity.

As to one thing time has proved him to have been entirely wrong. He did not believe that the then comparatively new divorce law would have much effect on France, and on French family life. I was amused when he remarked that all marriages where money played a great part were a survival of the time when a man bought his wife. He lamented the fact that brain workers are apt to have small families, and added that as regarded his own country it was to the peasantry that the world must look for the workers and the thinkers of the future.

He was kind enough to ask me to go and see him again, and I did so on two other occasions.

XVI

WHEN in Paris for, say, a week, I always went to the play
two or three times. I have always had a passionate love of and
interest in the theatre, and everything connected with the theatre. Most Parisians are constant playgoers, a fact the French Government has long recognized by allowing members of the public
to go free of charge on certain days of the year to the two state-
subsidized theatres.

In my young days, going to a play in Paris was an extremely
uncomfortable experience. One had to run the gauntlet of the
generally hideous, and very fat, old crones, whose excuse for a
tip was that of providing the playgoer with a footstool. The
public protested angrily against this imposition, but nothing was
done to put an end to it; and I remember my cousin, Marcel
Ballot, observing that some day the audience would suddenly
rise and murder these *ouvreuses,* as they were called. He said this
to me just after the patient suburban public, having put up with
the trains always being late, and the ticket collectors always being rude, suddenly became what is called in France *moutons en-
ragés,* and broke everything that was breakable, with their hands
and sticks, in the great station of Saint Lazare. After that had
happened, the trains became, for a time at any rate, more punc-
tual, and the ticket collectors more civil.

There was something else, and from my point of view it was
something very disagreeable, connected with seeing a play in
Paris. The performance always lasted till midnight, and sometimes even later than midnight. There were few cabs, and the

omnibuses were taken by assault. So I generally had to walk all the way back to the small hotel on the other side of the river where I then stayed. However, I was very strong, and quite fearless, and I was never spoken to, or molested. The exciting adventures which some of my young English friends described, never happened to me. A girl I knew who was studying art, told me she hardly ever went out without some stranger claiming her acquaintance. Indeed one day a man, who turned out to be a prince, after following her for a long time, caught up with her half-way across the Boulevard des Italiens and, seizing her arm, fervently exclaimed, *"Vient que je t'embrasse, mon petit chou!"*

I had one strange, disquieting, and to me painful experience. Through Mrs. Augustus Craven, whose book, *Le Récit d'une sœur,* was at one time world famous, I came in touch with her nephew, Comte Albert de Mun, the enthusiastic Christian socialist. At the time I was writing a paper on contemporary French politics, and he and his wife asked me to lunch. I felt interested at meeting him, for he was a son of the girl who is the most delightful character in *Le Récit d'une sœur.* After lunch I had a most delightful talk with him; and, as I was leaving, he said he thought I ought to see Paul de Cassagnac. He added, "I will give you a note for him. We are at the opposite poles as regards politics, but we are slightly acquainted, and both members of the French Parliament." He wrote the note, and I made an appointment to see the well-known Imperialist. I was aware Monsieur de Cassagnac was something of a fire-eater, and a noted duellist; apart from these two facts, I knew nothing about him.

I had scarcely sat down in his office, for he was editing a paper, when he suddenly said in what I can only describe as a ferocious voice, "I ask you to confess what it is Albert de Mun wishes me to tell you in order that you can transmit it to him?" I at once got up and answered, I hope in as ferocious a tone as his own, that I was not seeing the Comte de Mun again, and that my only reason for having wished to see either de Mun, or de Cassagnac, was because I was about to write an article for an English review concerning the French political situation. My attitude evidently surprised him, and he proceeded to make me somewhat cold excuses. I then exclaimed how terrible a thing I thought it that such a Frenchman as I believed him to be, should have supposed that such a Frenchman as I knew Albert de Mun to be, should have tried, by underhand means, to find out something— I could not imagine what it could be—Paul de Cassagnac wished should remain secret.

He made no reply to that, but I hope and believe he felt rather ashamed, perhaps foolish, too, as the party to which he belonged had few spokesmen in Europe, and he may have dimly apprehended that it would have been to his advantage to put his views before me. He accompanied me through his office, down to the front door, and saw me into a *fiacre*.

That was my only unpleasant experience during the years when I frequently went to Paris with a view to work. Indeed there was one great difference in the London and the Paris of that day. In London it was still regarded as unfitting in some quarters, and amusing and absurd in others, that a young woman should be doing the kind of journalism on which I was then engaged. I was never confronted with that attitude in Paris; there the men and women I went to see, seemed to think it quite natural I should be gathering material for English papers. No one appeared to feel my sex had anything to do with the way of life I chose to lead. But the French have always respected the profession of letters. Years later, I wished to see the Morgue, in order to place there the scene of a novel. By that time, the Morgue could only be entered by those who had reason to suppose that they would recognize in one of the bodies, a relation or friend who had disappeared. Before I left London, I was assured that unless I would go through the lugubrious farce of pretending some one belonging to me was missing, I should not obtain a permit. I naturally refused to think of doing such a thing. On arriving in Paris, I went to the British Consul, and even to the American Consul. Both these gentlemen declared they could give me no help, and further observed there was not the slightest hope of my being allowed to visit the Morgue. The same thing was told me by one of the correspondents of *The Times*. At last I went to the Prefecture of Police. There I explained I was a novelist, and writing a scene I wished to lay in the Morgue. Without even asking me to prove what I said was true, I was at once given the permit.

To return to the French theatre. It was with pleasure I received, owing to an introduction from my cousin Marcel, a note from Sardou asking me to call on him in his Paris house. One reason why I so longed to see him was that I had been told of his unique knowledge of what may be called the human nature side of the French Revolution. It is now known that Lenôtre was much indebted to Sardou with regard to the series of volumes called *Vieilles maisons, vieux papiers*. But apart from that side of his many-sided, cultivated character, Sardou was one of the most amusing and original men of letters it was my good fortune to meet during the early 'nineties. When I knew him, at the height of his success as a playwright, he was about sixty, though mentally he might have been thirty, and physically any age, for he was very thin and small, his face and expression recalling Voltaire in old age.

Everything in this world has to be paid for, and Sardou's unwise assent to writing what he himself called *de grosses machines,* to enable Sarah Bernhardt to act in countries where the French language is but little known, destroyed his reputation as a playwright in England and America. This was especially true of England, where even now there are allusions to Sardoudoolum, a word devised by Bernard Shaw. It was the more unfortunate, as Sardou did not write those melodramas to make more money—no writer was ever more indifferent to the piling up of money—but because he had what he called a *faible* for Sarah, and the writing of a *grosse machine* was to him child's play. I wonder if Mr. Shaw is acquainted with the plays which still delight intelligent French audiences—*Nos intimes,* which hardly dates after eighty years, *La Famille Benoîton, Nos bons villageois. La Famille Benoîton* is far the best of the many satirical pictures of the Second Empire likely to survive. Before it could be played, Sardou had a fierce battle with the Censor, and it caused such a stir that it was acted, at the wish of the Empress Eugenie, at Compiègne. But it so shocked and angered her that she declared Sardou must be a malicious devil, and she told a friend she could not believe such people as he had invented existed. *Rabagas,* produced just after the Franco-Prussian War, might have been written any time in the last twenty years. It gave a terrible portrait of a certain type of unscrupulous, dishonest, yet popular demagogue, and so it was naturally violently attacked by every member of the Government. A group of French parliamentarians made a strong effort to have it suppressed. But they failed, and it was said that had it been put on in three Paris theatres, they could all have been filled every night during its run. *Thermidor* also roused a passion of anger and rage among the politicians, and a Cabinet Council was called at which it was decided that the play should be suspended, on the pretence it was an insult to the French nation.

The French divorce law had hardly been passed before Sardou saw the chance divorce would give French dramatists. The first of the innumerable divorce plays written and produced was *Divorçons,* which remains one of the funniest comedies acted on the French stage. All these facts, and they are facts, surely prove that there was a good deal to be said for Sardoudoolum.

He told me that even as a child, he had been absorbed and fascinated in that period of French history which had followed the

Fall of the Bastille, and that whenever in his early youth he had met any one who had lived in, or just after, the Revolution, he had questioned, and cross-questioned, him or her. He said it was oftener a woman than a man, as women live longer than men. All through his life he had been willing to take a long journey to see, say, a grandson of some one who had been guillotined, and who was said to own letters which had been written during the Revolution. He kept a book in which he put down everything he heard connected with Louis the Sixteenth. He learnt from an old woman, whose grandmother had been one of Marie Antoinette's confidential maids, that there were two secret attempts to murder Marie Antoinette before she and the King left Versailles for ever. One of the men who intended to kill her was found hidden in her bath.

I once asked him who was the most interesting person he had met connected with the Great Revolution. Without a moment's hesitation he answered, "Madame Lebas." She was at a children's party where he was as a boy, and though she was then an old woman, she danced with him. It was then considered very bad taste to mention the Revolution, and those who were in any way connected with one of the men who had played a part in the huge convulsion, were apt to change their names. All the same, young Sardou at once began putting all kinds of questions to the widow of the man all those present at the party would have regarded as the infamous Lebas. She answered his questions readily, and only showed emotion when he ventured to mention Robespierre. She then reddened, and exclaimed that no man had ever been more cruelly misunderstood.

I spent an afternoon seeing Sardou rehearse one of his plays. But though I cannot remember what play it was I can see him now skipping about the large bare stage; completely dominating the actors and actresses; and, I suppose without knowing it, acting every part himself far better than either actor or actress could hope to do. But this no doubt was owing to the fear in which they held him, for he had a sharp malicious tongue, and, as he once told me, made a point of knowing none of his interpreters outside the green-room. The only thing which embittered his life, and to which he would return with lively anger, was the way in which, according to him, the plots of some of his plays, indeed whole acts, had been stolen by foreign playwrights. He was probably right, for though poorly esteemed, the plot mind is a rare type of creative mind, and he certainly possessed it to an outstanding extent. He once exclaimed, "I do not go to history for my plots, as did our great Dumas; mine are all extracted from my poor little head!"

No side of life left him indifferent. He liked to recall that, when he was sixteen, he had the good fortune (from his point of view) to be walking in the Faubourg Saint Honoré when the body of the Duchesse de Praslin had just been discovered, and he joined the crowd of men and women which forced its way into the splendid house which belonged to the poor woman's father, Marshal Sebastiani. He even caught a glimpse of her murderer, the Duc de Praslin.

There must have been a romantic side to Sardou's nature, for though he was noted among his friends and fellow writers for his good sense, he expended what were then all his savings—money he had earned with so much labour and such difficulty—on the purchase of a small eighteenth-century château at Marly-le-roi, which was in so bad a condition it had practically to be rebuilt. I wished I had had the courage to ask him to allow me to go and see him there. It was fairly near to La Celle Saint Cloud, and I had always felt a great curiosity about the place, for all sorts of stories were current when I was a child, as to the splendour of the gardens, and especially as to the alarming appearance of the rows of huge sphinxes which lined each side of the carriage-way to the front door of the house.

Frenchmen and Frenchwomen are singularly individual. I have never known two French people who were in the least alike, and that though they might have come from the same world, have had the same upbringing, be of the same age and sex, and following the same way of life.

Two men could hardly have been more different than Sardou and Dumas *fils*. Yet not only were they playwrights who often chose their characters from a similar strata of society, their lives covered much the same space of time; they were both Parisians through and through, and frequented much the same world. Considering how unlike they were, to me it is an interesting fact that they held one strong belief in common, for each of them was a convinced spiritualist, and believed in communion with the dead.

Sardou struck me as a very happy man; the younger Dumas as sombre, at odds with human society, and for ever secretly seeking for something which eluded him. His whole life, I feel sure, was powerfully affected by the fact of his illegitimate birth. Yet no man so circumstanced had less reason to remember it, and it would have been forgotten, indeed hardly known, had he not himself constantly recalled it. That he did so was the more inexplicable as he was excessively reserved in speech, and even secretive in manner.

I first met Dumas *fils* in the house of a lady to whom he was at the time deeply attached, yet he treated her as he might have done a slight acquaintance. She had told me he was at his best with young people, and I soon sensed it amused and surprised him that I knew at any rate something of his work, and had read certain of what were then the famous prefaces he had written, or was writing, to his plays. These prefaces, as he once said to me with a smile, were more admired than his dramas; but that was naturally only true of the thinking public. He was pleased at my intimate knowledge of his father's novels, for the older he grew, the more proud and devoted he became to the memory of that prodigious and prodigal genius. This was again the stranger when it is recalled that in the preface to his play *The Natural Son*, Dumas *fils* said that, were he a law-giver, he would give a sentence of ten years to any man over twenty-one who had an illegitimate child! Indeed he more than once publicly stated he thought such a man far more wicked than an ordinary murderer.

Even I realized the strong streak of violence in his nature, and yet, outwardly, as my cousin Marcel once told me, his manner was the most glacial of any man in the Parisian society of his day; and when he came into a room where there were only three or four people, every one felt chilled, even frightened. Not that he went much into a world of men and women where almost every view held by him with passionate conviction was regarded with suspicion and distaste. When I knew him, he had a fierce, though always quietly expressed, contempt for the Republican régime. He once declared in print that régime had produced a society of men and women *poitrinaire et bâtarde*. He also had an intense horror of war, and the one cheerful conviction held by him was that the end of warfare, as a way of settling international quarrels, was in sight. In 1940 he would have shared the views of Marshal Pétain. Indeed, just after the end of the Franco-Prussian War, he wrote a few lines which recall almost word for word the first broadcast of Marshal Pétain. In it he exalted family life, advised the France of 1871 to endure privation, to be modest, patient, and find salvation in hard work. I once heard him make angry fun of the words *"Liberté, Égalité, Fraternité."*

There were times when he talked as if he belonged, in a real sense, to the Catholic Church, yet he refused to allow the two daughters to whom he was devoted to be given any form of religious teaching. This distressed and shocked their mother, Princess Narishkine, who was Greek Orthodox, and was one of the reasons why Dumas and she separated. Yet, to the amazement of his friends, the two girls were brought up by him in the strictest and most conventional way. Neither of them was allowed to see one of their father's plays before they married, and he must have shared the views of the abbé who, when asked what he thought of dancing, replied that as far as he could see it was either boring, indecent, or both. Colette and Jeannine Dumas were not allowed to accept invitations to the *bals blancs* which played so pleasant a part in the lives of French girls of their kind. When Jeannine fell in love with, and became engaged to, a young officer who belonged to one of the old Legitimist families, his mother discovered the girl had never been baptized. So against her father's will she was christened, but her future in-laws were vexed Dumas chose Princess Mathilde to be her godmother. The old Princess, a niece of Napoleon, so admired not only the plays, but also the social theories of Dumas *fils* that, as she put it herself, she compelled him to become her friend. She did not add what was true, that many of those who composed her circle resented his presence, for he always said exactly what he thought, and his theories as to women and their place in the world were much resented. His loudly expressed horror of adultery aroused derision, a derision justified by the fact that he did not practise what he preached. But after the love affair in early youth with Marie Duplessis (who inspired *La Dame aux camélias*), he never allowed himself to fall in love again with an actress. It may, I feel, be said that no novelist, playwright, or even philanthropist, was ever as preoccupied with women, their wrongs, their rights, and every side of their lives, as was Dumas *fils*. Each of his famous prefaces is an embroidery of some feminine theme. He at once loved and hated all womanhood, and, to my indignation, once spoke to me with contempt of those men who wished women to have the vote.

I should have expected him to have disliked George Sand, whom I had always been taught to revere, because of my mother's enthusiastic admiration for her. But her splendid generosity of nature, and her *bonhomie,* had conquered what must have been at the time a very embittered young man; and he spoke to me of her with an affection and respect which touched and surprised me.

As is, I think, always the way with a man (or woman) of strong and violent nature, Dumas *fils* possessed some ardently devoted friends of both sexes. A man who had been fond of his father, and had become fond of Dumas *fils,* left him a charming house at Marly-le-roi, and there he spent a great deal of his life during his last years.

After the death of his Russian wife, from whom he parted many years before her death, he married again. His second wife was a widow, and daughter of a well-known actor. They were married six months before his death, and when he was dying he told his younger daughter those months had been the happiest months of his life.

I once had what was to me an absorbing conversation concerning his methods of work, and the art of playwriting. Plot was nothing, the central idea everything, and he invented characters who could express the idea he wished to present and to force on the attention of his audience. Once a play had been blocked out in his mind, he wrote it in three weeks. But that was only a rough draft, and he spent many months in expanding and altering the first version.

Unlike practically all his contemporaries and fellow writers, he led a simple, austere life. He began each day by drinking a glass of milk. He ate very little, and lived largely on vegetables. Few educated Frenchmen of that day, unless they were country gentlemen, were walkers, but when he was living at Marly, he went every day for a long solitary walk.

The last time I saw Dumas *fils* was at the unveiling of a monument to Émile Augier. I was shocked by the change in his appearance, but I was told by some one present he was extremely anxious just then, as one of his sons-in-law was supposed to be dying. He made a fine speech in honour of his one-time rival, and he lingered on talking to some of the people there. But that same evening he fell ill, and only lived a few days.

Instead of putting in his will his wish to be buried with either his father or mother, as both his daughters had expected him to do, he arranged to be buried either at Père-Lachaise or at Montmartre; and the friend in whose house I had first met him told me that in each of those cemeteries was lying the body of a woman he had loved. Neither of them was Marie Duplessis.

The French Government generally undertakes all the expenses connected with the funeral of a noted man, and a military guard of honour is always present. Dumas *fils* was naturally aware of this custom, and he actually put in his will the phrase, "*pas de soldats.*"

XVII

I WROTE for hours of each day during my visits to Paris, and as I disliked sitting in what was nearly always a very cold bedroom, I spent a great deal of my time on the ground floor of an old building in one of the quiet squares on the left bank of the Seine. There was housed, what did not exist in any other part of Paris, a really good circulating library, as well as a large room to which the entrance fee was fifty centimes, and where could be read practically every newspaper published in France. This reading-room was a pleasure and resource to me; I think it must have been run by some eccentric literary man or woman, for it cannot have paid its way. Few people ever went there, though now and again an obvious peasant would creep in, with an alarmed, furtive expression on his face, to try and find the local paper of his *pays*.

I only occasionally had time to see my relations; but they all lived, by then, far from the centre of Paris, and the horse-drawn omnibuses seemed to crawl along. All the same, in a sense my happiest hours in Paris were spent with my own people. I enjoyed most of all being with Aunt Lily, and the charming setting of her old-fashioned sitting-room brought back not only my childhood at La Celle Saint Cloud, but the cloudless period, never to return, when I had believed all men and women to be good and kind. During the years which had drifted by between those days and the present time, I had had good reason to find how false had been my then belief. When with my aunt I kept this knowledge to myself for, young as I still was, I well knew

she had always belonged to the sheltered, stable world of womanhood; the world my mother, through no fault of her own, had
lost, while quite unaware she was doing so, as she also was of the
effect that loss would have on each of her children. To the end
of her ninety-four years of life she was ever being puzzled and
surprised by meeting with the truth of that fearful saying, "Woe
to the vanquished." Although in theory she was keenly aware of
the injustice and even cruelty shown to those, especially women,
who fall behind in the race, in practice she thought it common
form that the strong should help the weak, and the happy the
miserable. Such had been the practice of certain of the friends of
her youth and middle age, Barbara Bodichon, Adelaide Procter,
Mary Merryweather, Mrs. Howitt, Lady Augusta Stanley—the
list is not a very long one. It was also the way and practice of the
three Frenchwomen with whom she became so closely associated
—her husband's mother and his two sisters. I had early had reason to know such conduct to be the exception, not the rule, in
this strange life, as also that victory only comes to the strong. In
the days of my youth I was strong, and so often victorious, yet
it was wonderfully pleasant, even in the midst of what had become a most interesting working life, to drift into what seemed,
in my early twenties, the quiet backwater where dwelt almost
every member of my own family.

I happened to be in Paris when the Étienne Sirys gave a ball.
That I, the only girl of them all, should not be among their
guests would have seemed unnatural indeed; and I, myself, had
a foolish childish longing to be there, especially as I knew it was
not to be a *bal blanc,* but a dance for grown-up people. But I
did not possess, even in England, any suitable frock. This was
at once realized by Aunt Lily, and she and Marcel begged me to
try and find something ready made which should be their gift.
I found at once a pale-pink tulle *robe de bal* for what, in English
money was three pounds, at the Bon Marché. I exhibited myself

in the ball dress to both the kind donors, and neither of them thought it conceivable the price had been as small as seventy-five francs. I convinced Aunt Lily, but Marcel lay in wait for me on the staircase, and told me in the *argot* of that day he knew I had kidded his simple-minded mother. He said I could not take him in, as he had sometimes bought an evening frock for a lady, and knew the very cheapest ball dress cost at least three hundred francs and, imperiously, he tried to stuff two hundred and fifty francs into my hand. I answered, I hope with spirit, that the lady to whom he had been so kind had kidded *him*.

Oh! how I enjoyed the Sirys' delightful ball of fifty years ago! All the more delightful as the then still little daughters of the host and hostess flitted about like pretty butterflies.

I was introduced that night to a woman I had always wished to meet. Madame Madeleine Lemaire had been for three decades the most celebrated of French flower-painters, and she was said to earn a yearly income of a hundred thousand francs (£4000), the equivalent to what double that sum would be to-day.

My interest in her personality was not owing to her celebrity, or to the amount of money she was said to earn. I wished to meet her because she was a fairly close relation of mine, for her father, Professor Coll, who had a chair in one of the southern universities, had been a second cousin of Hilaire Belloc.

Madeleine Coll must have been something of an infant prodigy, for when only fifteen she exhibited a portrait at the Salon which attracted favourable notice. My grandfather gave her an introduction to Charles Chaplin, the Empress Eugenie's favourite portrait-painter, and she worked for two years in his studio, becoming his pet pupil. When she was eighteen, she made an unhappy marriage, and two years later horrified her provincial friends and neighbours by leaving her husband, and settling with her baby girl in Paris. Acting on Chaplin's advice, she devoted herself to flower-painting; yet she generally exhibited one or

more portraits at the Salon each year, and she drew illustrations
for books. Those of the first edition of *L'Abbé Constantin* keep
her name alive in the hearts of French bibliophiles. What stands
out in my memory is a delightful water-colour sketch of Marcel
Ballot in fancy dress.

Though she was fifty, she had retained, when I met her, a remarkable air of youth, and did not seem much older than her
daughter, Suzette. She did not look a strong woman, but her
vitality must have matched her industry. She built herself a house
in the Parc Monceau quarter of Paris, just before that quarter
became the fashion. There she entertained on a considerable
scale, giving afternoon and evening receptions which were attended by what was then called *Tout Paris,* and often organizing
private theatricals in a large hall which had been copied from
that in an historic château.

She asked me to one of her noted afternoon parties, and I was
astonished at the luxury in which she evidently lived, and at the
varied company she kept. But I felt no desire to know her better.
The judgements of thoughtful youth are apt to be harsh judgements, and I resented her complete neglect of Madame Swanton
Belloc and, later, of the surviving daughter of a man who, as she
herself told me, had done everything to help and encourage her,
when she was an unknown art-student in Paris.

It was during this visit to Paris I experienced for the first time
the kind of delight—it might have been called ecstasy—I suppose
fine music now and again gives to music's votaries. The same
feeling was only once again induced in me—this was when I saw
for the first time the Russian Ballet.

I owed what remains in my mind as one of the two most
memorable evenings in my life to my cousin, Marcel Ballot.
Although I did not know it, the whole of artistic Europe was beginning to be stirred and excited by the performance of a series
of shadow pictures which owed their being to a caricaturist called

Caran d'Ache. The fact *L'Épopée* had been produced at Le Chat Noir, a cabaret in Montmartre, placed it out of bounds for the kind of Frenchwomen with whom I was then acquainted. But this taboo did not last long, and during the year which followed, I think it reasonable to say that every *Parisienne* familiar with the history of France was taken to see that which brought alive the Napoleonic legend. As time went on, men and women journeyed from every country in the world to see *L'Épopée,* and it had a curious fascination for the then royal personages of Europe. Among those who came to Paris specially to see the shadow play was the Prince of Wales, later Edward the Seventh; and every one of the younger German and Scandinavian princes came to see it. But all this was to happen after I had been to one of the early performances.

I knew nothing of what we were going to see; but being taken out by Marcel always meant for me a happy and an exciting evening, for in every sense his nonsense suited my nonsense; and any show which pleased his fastidious taste was certain to please mine too.

As our *fiacre* breasted the steep dark streets leading to Montmartre, he told me something of the Chat Noir and its owner, a showman of genius named Rodolphe Salis, who had begun life as an unsuccessful painter, and as a writer of topical humorous verse.

While living in Montmartre, Salis heard that the good-will of a café called Le Chat Noir was going for a few hundred francs. He put down the money, and set his mind to making the café a success. He began with a mild *succès de scandale,* by dressing up his waiters in the green-and-black uniform worn by the members of the French Academy. The Academicians angrily protested at being turned into derision; but their protest simply gave the Chat Noir an advertisement, and a great many people who had never had the chance of being present at a séance of the

Academy spent an evening at Montmartre to see waiters in the guise of Immortals. I had been fairly often to the Academy, so these dummy members of the Forty did not interest me.

But Marcel's account of what I supposed would be an historical play, with each character shown as a shadow, aroused my curiosity. I felt disappointed when we went into a long narrow hall, and I saw how small was the white screen across which I knew what some of those round me called *ombres chinoises* were to be thrown. But when came the first scene, I was at once carried away as if into another dimension, and felt myself living through the years when France dominated the then civilized world, with the exception of what was still Shakespeare's little isle set in a silver sea. Even now, when I read of any phase of Napoleon's life, what leaps into my mind is one of the scenes I saw that evening at Le Chat Noir.

Without waiting to obtain a commission, I decided I would get in touch with, and write an account of, the genius to whom the world owed *L'Épopée*.

I found Caran d'Ache living in a small house in a quiet street near the Bois de Boulogne. He looked, talked, and acted, more like an Englishman than a Frenchman, for he was tall, slight, active, and fond of every form of outdoor life. He and his young Russian wife were simple and attractive in manner, and I was destined, after our first meeting, to spend now and again a happy hour with them both, and he gave me several charcoal drawings of Napoleon.

The real name of this caricaturist was Poiré. His great-grandfather had been one of Napoleon's staff officers, and had accompanied the Emperor to Moscow; fortunately for himself he was wounded, and so did not perish in the Great Retreat. He was taken into a private house, nursed, and kindly treated; then he fell in love with the daughter of the house, married her, and settled down in Russia. But neither he nor his descendants gave up their name of Poiré, or their French nationality. So when one of his great-grandsons, Emmanuel Poiré, decided to be a painter, he naturally went to Paris to study. The young man made no effort to evade conscription, and not till after he had done his military service in the ranks did he settle down to paint. But he was very poor, and the military painter, Détaille, realizing Poiré's special gift, told him that while painters were many, there were very few humorous artists, and he strongly advised him to follow what was evidently his natural bent. Though disappointed, Poiré took the older man's advice, and adopted the name of Caran d'Ache (which he told me was Russian for lead pencil), and he soon had as much work as he could do. But Napoleon had always been his hero, and suddenly he decided to draw a pictorial life of that great man. He had seen at the Chat Noir a comic interlude produced by moving shadows across a white screen, and this was the genesis of what Caran d'Ache already intended to call *L'Épopée*: the central figure, that which he intended should dominate every scene, being naturally that of Napoleon. Putting everything aside, he spent many months in making four thousand separate drawings of *la grande armée*. Then he cut out each drawing, and pasted it on a piece of zinc.

He then took his four thousand little silhouettes to Rodolphe Salis, and together they worked out the thirty scenes of *L'Épopée*. The scene that gave them the most trouble was that showing the Retreat from Moscow, and it was by far the finest and the most imaginative of them all. They produced an amazing effect of reality by showing the march, in single file, of men, horses, and every kind of military coach and wagon, moving slowly on wide fields of snow, and across frozen rivers.

In a sense I am sorry, in another sense I am glad, that I was not taken to the two shadow pictures that followed *L'Épopée*. I I should have regretted seeing what might have disturbed my memory of *L'Épopée*. Yet it would have amused me to have seen Caran d'Ache's vision of the Paris of the early 'nineties which he called *Bois de Boulogne*. And his shadow picture of the great Russian wastelands, *Les Steppes,* was, I believe, as fine as *L'Épopée*. Though he was begged to do more work of the same kind, he went back to caricature.

Some of his political drawings show a very different side of his character from that which appeared in his shadow pictures. I own one caricature which, in view of what has happened since, gives a sinister impression. It is called "European Concert," and shows the then Great Powers arranged as members of a band about to start playing. The German bandsman is beating the big drum; the Spanish mediæval-looking cavalier vaguely recalls the figure in history which he once told me counted, next to Napoleon, most in the imagination of Caran d'Ache, that is, Don Quixote. Britannia, conductor of the band, puts out a warning hand to France, drawn as a naughty-looking little girl, and exclaims, "Wait! you have started two bars too soon."

I was much drawn to the work of the French caricaturists, and I once pleased Edmond de Goncourt by expressing my enthusiasm for Gavarni. I came in touch with Chéret, and at one time possessed a considerable number of his fine posters. Hilaire Belloc had known and much admired the then little thought-of great artist, Daumier, and one of my French cousins had some drawings given by Daumier to my grandfather.

Through Yvette Guilbert, whom I grew to know quite well, I met Willette. Yvette Guilbert, apart from her gift as singer and *diseuse,* was a brilliant and cultivated woman. When she came to London, in the days of her fame, I saw her frequently, and a few years ago I spent a delightful hour in her company. She wished to make a film of a novel of mine called *What Really Happened*. But she desired to alter the leading character from a young, into an old, woman, and I refused her offer.

Even in my early twenties I was intensely interested in every form of art, and it was a real misfortune for me that during my many visits to Paris I had no chance of meeting such painters as Manet and Monet—to name but two whose work means much to me. Of the nineteenth-century portrait-painters, Ingres so pleased me that, as a young woman, I would go far, even out of Paris, to see pictures painted by him.

A word to Oscar Wilde (he and his wife were among the friends I had made early in my London life) would have opened to me the whole of the advanced French world of art and thought. But I do not remember ever asking for an introduction, excepting in connection with my work.

I never met Condor, but I was once offered one of his beautiful fans for a hundred francs, but I did not feel I could spend what was then four pounds on something which would only be a pleasure to myself. I constantly heard of Mr. and Mrs. Whistler. But there again, though a slight effort on my.part would have made me come into contact with them, it never occurred to me I could make that effort.

I was only allowed by my editors to suggest the name or names of a Frenchman or Frenchwoman already known in England. This was a misfortune for me from every point of view. Had it been otherwise, I should have become acquainted with painters who have survived in a way in which those then "in the news" failed in doing. Aunt Lily, who, although she seldom spoke of art, only had that one interest in her life, though she had long since given up her studio, would now and again take me to see the work of a painter who was looked at with a curious mixture of contempt and distrust by the established men whose position was akin to the British Royal Academicians. She delighted in the work of Fantin-Latour and Renoir; and she knew the dealers who were beginning to interest themselves in the younger painters. I spent a couple of hours in one of Julian's famous studios; I think he had at that time three, but only one bore his name. He suggested I should pretend to be a new pupil, for in no other way could I have seen the students at work, without their taking notice of a stranger. The experience is impressed on my mind because there had been a time, in my very early girlhood, when I had thought of being a painter.

The readers of the sort of papers and magazines for whom I was then writing did not care for those whose fame lay in the future. My editors were interested, so far as they were interested in anything French, in those painters whose names were popularized by the great art publishers. Thus, when it became known that Goupil was about to spend twenty thousand pounds on publishing a book dealing with the French Army from the year of the Fall of the Bastille, which was to contain five hundred illustrations from drawings or paintings by Détaille, I was at once asked to find out all about him—and the *Strand Magazine* commissioned me to write an article on the man who was then considered the greatest living battle-painter in the world.

I have retained an affectionate memory of this agreeable and generous Parisian. It can be truly said that when he consented to grant me an interview, he was one of the three or four most popular artists in Europe, and so nothing I was likely to write could in any way benefit him. Yet he not only gave me two hours of his time, he offered me some valuable introductions. Détaille came of a well-known military family, and he had fought as a youth in the Franco-Prussian War. He took great personal interest in the panorama of the battle at Champigny, where he had himself fought as a private. He was regarded as Meissonier's successor; but though his reputation has not remained on the same level, he had far more imagination than his master. When I wrote a children's book, in the autumn of 1914, called *Told in Gallant Deeds,* I chose as frontispiece his picture called "Le Rêve," which shows a mass of sleeping men on the edge of a battlefield, while above in the clouds the fight goes on.

I was naïvely surprised to find with what intense horror Détaille regarded war. On two occasions the French Government forbade a picture of his to be exhibited in the Salon, because they considered it as too horrible to be shown. Yet Détaille was the only man, during those years, I heard speak with sympathy of Déroulède, and he quoted with passionate admiration the verse:

> En avant! Tant pis pour qui tombe;
> La mort n'est rien.
> Vive la tombe
> Quand le pays en sort vivant.
> En avant!

I was also asked by the *Strand Magazine* to write an account of Jules Verne. As children, my brother and I delighted in his books, especially in *Round the World in Eighty Days* and *Five Weeks in a Balloon*. So I felt pleased when I received a kind note saying he was willing to see me; and I spent the day at Amiens, where I found Jules Verne in a typical French provincial town house, built round a courtyard. Though he and his wife had celebrated their golden wedding, he did not look sixty.

I was astonished to learn that his ambition as a young man was to be a playwright. He had actually written a comedy in collaboration with Dumas *fils*, with whom he seemed to have remained on terms of friendship. In the present day he would have become a millionaire through the adaptation of his novel *Michel Strogoff*. After we had talked for a considerable time in a drawing-room which was obviously kept for only occasional use, I asked him if he would mind showing me his study. To my surprise he took me up to a tiny room of which the furniture consisted of a narrow iron bed, a wooden armchair, and a small writing-table on which stood two busts, the one of Molière and the other of Shakespeare.

I little thought a day would come when, like Jules Verne, I

would begin story-writing at five in the morning. But, unlike me, he always got up and dressed before he started work and, also unlike me, he never wrote a line after his eleven o'clock *déjeuner*.

But though he did all his writing in this curious little room, there was on the same floor a large library, in which stood an immense table where lay what appeared to me every scientific and geographical magazine published in the world. His favourite author—in this like many Frenchmen of his generation—was Sir Walter Scott; and my heart warmed to him when he told me how fond he had always been of *The Swiss Family Robinson*.

Now that both Jules Verne, and the old lady who showed me such courtesy that day have both been dead for many years, I feel I may tell the story of how their marriage came about. It was told me long afterwards, by the only French writer I ever came across who had known them, for they lived quite out of the literary world.

To the distress of his parents, as a young man Jules Verne made up his mind never to marry. He was completely absorbed in writing poetry and plays, and his only intimate friend was a man of much his own age whom he had known all his life. After a while, this friend married, and went to live in a far-distant part of France, and so the tie between the two was loosened. But within three years, his one-time close friend died, and Jules Verne journeyed to be present at his funeral. The young widow was in such a state of anguish that she was unable to follow the universal custom of walking behind the coffin. She stayed in the house, and Jules Verne felt so concerned at her state, that he remained with her. She was the lady who in due course lived to celebrate her golden wedding with her fellow mourner. She had had a child by her first husband, and to this stepson Jules Verne was devoted, and he left to him what was for those days his large fortune.

XVIII

DURING the early 'nineties I came in touch, and became on really friendly terms, with a group of remarkable Frenchwomen, perhaps I ought to say *Parisiennes*. They were extremely different the one from the other, and recalled in no way the women of my own family. The most kindly and most generous-natured of them all, was Madame Juliette Adam. She was so famous in her day that a Paris street was given her maiden name, and she lived there, in the rue Juliette Lamber, in a modest-looking house, and gave most interesting parties. These were attended by many more men than women, partly because she was regarded as having considerable influence with certain members of the Government. She had been for a long time Gambetta's political Egeria, but she had broken with him when it became known he had made a secret visit to Germany in order to have an interview with Bismarck.

Madame Adam was a middle-aged woman when I first knew her, and made no effort to look a day younger than she was, though in her youth she must have been beautiful. After an unhappy early marriage, she left her husband, and became a kind of adopted daughter of George Sand. Then, after a while, she joined her life with that of Monsieur Adam, whom she described to me, with an emotion never shown by her except on that one occasion, as one of the very few absolutely worthy and honest men with whom she had ever come in contact. They ultimately married, and after his death she lived, as regarded her private life, the ordinary existence of a respectable French widow, and I

never heard of her having had a lover. She always made me welcome to her weekly gatherings, which was truly good of her, as I must have been at least twenty years younger than any one there. On two occasions she invited me to an enchanting *fête champêtre* in her country house, L'Abbaye de Gif, which had been built on the site of a mediæval monastery. She owned and edited *La Nouvelle Revue,* and she must have had a remarkable flair, for she discovered writers as different as Bourget, Loti, and Maupassant. Indeed she is said to have chosen Loti's pen-name, after she read in manuscript the novel in which that name occurred. It was at one of these garden parties I met both Loti and Maupassant. I had with Maupassant a curious conversation, during which he expressed great interest in English eighteenth-century literature. He regarded *Tom Jones* as one of the great novels of the world; but he said to me, "All the same, *Tom Jones* is a book you must not look into till you are married."

Madame Adam called Maupassant *mon bon taureau.* He really looked like a bull, for he had a short, strong, sturdy figure, and a curiously-shaped, almost square, face. I was vaguely aware that he had been the pupil, almost the adopted son, of Flaubert and, as I look back, I feel I was foolish not to speak to him of Flaubert, for whom I had, and have, not only a passionate admiration, but inasmuch as a woman can have such a feeling for a man she has never met, a warm affection. As for Loti, my mother put him among the first writers of that time. Both *Mon frère Yves* and *Pêcheurs d'Islande* had been put into my hands when I was little more than a child, to the shocked surprise of some old family friends who had happened to come to La Celle Saint Cloud, and found me reading one of these two moving and noble books.

I was disappointed in Loti. He had a cold, abrupt manner, and moved about in the merry crowd on the lawns of L'Abbaye de Gif, looking like a scoffing ghost, rather than a man of flesh and

blood. He was the only Frenchman I ever heard of, who disliked Paris. I suspect he hated the kind of Parisians with whom Madame Adam brought him in touch. His voice only softened when he spoke to her, calling her *ma patronne* with an affectionate inflection in his squeaky, high-pitched voice.

By far the most original, eccentric, and, in every sense of the word, brilliant woman writer I have known, was Gyp, in private life the Comtesse de Martel. She was a great-granddaughter of Mirabeau's brother, Riquetti, and was justifiably proud of having been born a Mirabeau. There was in her character something of the great man's violence of character, though this was far more shown in her drawings than in her novels. The first time I was in her house, I noticed that the most prominent object in her sitting-room was a screen covered with savage caricatures of the Frenchmen then composing the French Government. In the centre of the screen was an excellent caricature of herself, engaged in electioneering in the seaside place she called in one of her books *Tigre-sur-Mer*. Certain of her drawings recall Gilray's coloured drawings.

She was entirely unlike the French women of her class and day, and she lived far from the centre of Paris, outside the fortifications. There she had a spacious house and large garden. She told me she could never have endured living in an *appartement*, as did all her friends and acquaintances.

She started her married life, when only eighteen, in a small garrison town, and there she felt so bored that she began writing to amuse herself, taking the people with whom she was then thrown, as models. Her first sketches—they could not be called stories—were sent by her to *La Vie Parisienne*, a paper she told me with glee could not then have been seen in the hands of any respectable young married woman without her character being thereby damaged. The sketches were accepted by return of post, and to her naïve surprise she was not only paid for them, but very

well paid. So she began saving, there and then, with a view to buying the half-ruined castle of Mirabeau, which hung like an eagle's nest on a hill high up above the Rhône. It had remained unaltered since the day Mirabeau was born there.

When I first knew her, she had three children, her two sons being just grown-up; but she still looked quite young, and spent every spare moment of her time riding, fishing, and walking. She was the first woman in France to own a motor car—and amid the jeers of her friends, she started one day driving it to Versailles. But she broke down half-way, and this so disgusted her, that for a long time she gave up her car, and used to drive, with relays of horses, by road to Mirabeau. She had once been nearly stifled in a long tunnel, and after that experience never entered a train again.

Like so many French girls of her generation, she had been brought up on Dickens, and she adopted the signature "Gyp" because Jip was the name of Dora's dog in *David Copperfield*.

Madame de Martel was a passionate politician, and she brought politics, whenever she could manage to do so, into her then immensely popular novels, which were all written in dialogue. She was the first anti-semite I had ever met, and I was amazed at the energy with which she denounced all Jewry, and the rage with which she accused the Jews of having brought every kind of misfortune on France. At the time I had never even met any French *Israélites*, as they were called in France. But my mother had known well members of the Goldsmid family, and she had what I can only call a real veneration, as well as affection, for Mr. David Mocatta, the Jewish scholar-philanthropist. When I was a little girl she had once taken me to see him as a great privilege, and so strong an admiration of this man had been instilled into me from childhood that when, years later, I made several close friends in the Jewish community, I always asked them questions concerning the work and personality of David Mocatta. So

Gyp's attitude both surprised and disturbed me.

Members of the French nobility have always spent a great deal of their time in shooting and hunting. But Madame de Martel had a horror of all blood sports, and one of the first things she said to me was that, though she did not, in principle, think at all well of the British, as she regarded them as being both hypocritical and smug, she admired, and subscribed to the funds of the Society for the Protection of Animals.

Much in advance of her time as regarded the education of both boys and girls, she thought the brains of young boys ought not to be over-stimulated, as was then, and still is, the French way. She also strongly advocated an out-of-doors life for all young people, and her sons were taught to swim and ride as soon as they could walk.

Gyp did not live to be old. She must have worn out what was a slight delicate frame. Following the example of George Sand, she wrote her novels after every other member of her household had gone to bed. She began writing at midnight, and went on till four in the morning; but she was up and dressed by eleven, starting each day with an hour's ride.

She signed her caricatures "Bob," and her best-known book, which is still read, for it contains an extremely vivid picture of a child, and a child's mind, she called *P'tit Bob*. Yet she wrote one serious—it might almost be called a desperately serious—novel. It is called *Un Raté* (A Wastrel). When I first met her, her mind was full of it, and that she came to write this story fell out in this wise.

A young man named Chambige, who had literary ambitions, and was something of a poet, called on her one day. He looked ill, was shabbily dressed, and said diffidently he had heard she was looking for a holiday tutor for her sons. She did not much like him, for she thought him affected and, to use her own word, *sournois,* that is sly. Still, she felt sorry for him, and consented to give him the holiday engagement. He went with her and her children to the seaside; but she soon found he was lazy, and though he would now and again compose a few verses, he never attempted to write even one article for an editor to whom she had given him an introduction. He refused to bathe, and even disliked walking, so she felt sorry she had engaged him as tutor to her boys.

Not long after, on opening a paper, she saw that what was described as a *crime passionnel* had just taken place in Algiers, and that Chambige was the central figure of the case. In due course the mysterious story excited interest and wide discussion all over Europe.

According to Chambige, he had been for some time the secret lover of a young married woman, though she had a husband and two children to whom she appeared to be devoted. When it became plain she and the man, some years younger than herself, would soon have to part, as Chambige had been given a post in Paris, they entered, if he was to be believed, on a suicide pact.

One morning, when the lady's husband was away from Algiers on business, she sent her children out into the garden to play, and began writing a letter to her mother. When half-way through the letter, she was told Chambige had called to see her, and she said he was to be shown in.

Her servant overheard the visitor offering to drive her to a country house some way from the town belonging to an absent relation of Chambige, with whom she was on friendly terms, and where she herself would occasionally go to see that everything was in order.

She left the letter to her mother half written, and drove off with the young man in an open *fiacre*. They went together into the villa, and the cabman, after waiting a long time, grew uneasy. Going into the house he finally came to a room where he saw the lady lying dead on a bed, with Chambige, slightly wounded, by her side.

The young man was tried for murder. Innumerable witnesses testified to the high regard in which was held the woman he said had been his mistress. Her husband told how devoted he and she had been to one another, and how she had at times made fun of the hysterical young Parisian with whose relations they had long been acquainted. Much as was to happen, many years later, with regard to the Dreyfus case, violent quarrels broke out in French families as to whether Chambige had been guilty of a frightful murder, or victim of a suicide pact.

The truth has never been known, and is unlikely ever to be known. Chambige was not able to produce a single letter from the unfortunate woman; but several of his friends swore to the fact he had spoken to them of a secret love affair, and of the anguish both he and his lover felt at their coming parting. On the morning of the day she was found dead, he had told two young men something terrible was about to happen. He was not sentenced to death, as half the French world had hoped, but he was condemned to a long term of imprisonment.

Gyp was so moved and excited by the strange affair, and so convinced of Chambige's bad faith, that she wrote *Un Raté* as an ordinary novel, and not in dialogue form, to show her large public that this time she was writing in a serious vein a book to vindicate a woman's honour.

Gyp had exceptionally brilliant, expressive eyes, and they seemed to darken when I mentioned *Un Raté*. "I felt," she exclaimed, "as if what happened to that woman might conceivably have happened to me, when I was young, giddy, and imprudent, though I assure you extremely virtuous!" She had actually thought of going to Algiers to give her view of Chambige's character.

The only writer I ever heard her mention was Anatole France. She seemed very fond both of him and his wife. They had consulted her as to a possible divorce; she spoke to me of the matter; then wrote me an urgent letter begging me to keep what she had said to myself, which I naturally did.

One of the traits in her odd character that made me like her, was the intelligent love she showed for her children. That her system of education had been a good system became clear when her younger son joined the band of famous explorers. As for the elder boy she loved so dearly, and who sat for the immortal *P'tit Bob*, he became the greatest French surgeon of his day. Men and women came to consult him from all over the world, and he worked untiringly for his country throughout the last war. During the twenty-two years that followed, in addition to fame came happiness. He married a beautiful woman and, until June 1940, the lot of no Frenchman could have been more enviable, for in addition to everything else, he had a delightful nature, and a host of friends. But the day the Germans entered Paris, de Martel killed himself.

Some time before I met Louise Michel, my mother wrote to a friend:

"I am so very glad Louise Michel is now on her way back to France, though the Parisians will never forgive her for having helped to fire, and so destroy, many splendid buildings. I, personally, regret by far the most the Hôtel de Ville, and the Belloc family still grieve over the destruction of the Cour des Comptes. The poor Empress Eugenie must have been heartbroken as to the Tuileries, and I fear she left there many objects dear to her heart.

"You ask me about the extreme Left. They are no different in France to what they are everywhere else, my dear. They are on the whole disinterested; possessed by a vision of the future; foreseeing what they think will be a perfect life a century hence; and faithful to their comrades. They live far apart from all ordinary conventionalities and decencies; yet to my thinking they are far truer, in many ways, than are many decent regular people. In my view they have always been the same, from Mirabeau downwards. I would not care to live with them, but I see all their good and noble qualities, and ten years ago I fought many battles with our well-placed French friends for those who were then called Communists."

What my mother wrote was true, especially of the women of Paris. They all hated Louise Michel, for the active part she had played in the Commune, and I recall one of my grandmother's younger friends saying she would like to see her torn to pieces. But when she benefited by the political amnesty which brought many Communists back to Paris, there was much interest felt in her personality in London philanthropic circles; and I was asked to write an account of her the next time I went to Paris. I had great difficulty in finding out where she lived, but I had acquaintances, even then, among all kinds of Parisians, and at last I procured her address.

She lived in what can only be described as a state of sordid poverty, on the garret floor of an old and filthy house in one of the narrow streets behind the Palais Royal. She was devoted to animals, and she had eight or nine cats, as well as a sickly monkey, in her bedroom. In spite of the noise and smell, we had an interesting talk, and I took a real liking to her. I wrote a long letter to my mother describing her surroundings and our talk. I did not say that the moment I stepped out into the street I had not only shaken myself vigorously, but also taken some flying leaps into the air.

In due course, Louise Michel started what may be called her old ways; and after her success in organizing a successful bakers' strike, she had to fly, disguised, to England, which was then the refuge of the hunted and proscribed. An account I had written of her after our first meeting had pleased her, and she had kept in touch with me. So the moment I knew she was in London, I went to see her, and remembering the way she had lived in Paris, I took her a nice dish of cold meat which, to my annoyance, she shared with the cats she had already had time to adopt. But the monkey, fortunately, had died. I found, with relief, that she was receiving a small allowance from Henri Rochfort. At that time Rochfort was living in a delightful house overlooking the Regent's Park, and she in one small room near Seven Dials. They had first made friends in one of the cages on the deck of a ship sailing for New Caledonia. He once told me she had then shown him great kindness, so I felt he might have given her enough money to live in humble comfort.

What touched me in Louise Michel was her passion of pity for everything alive which happened to be suffering or unfortunate, from a deserted cat to an unwanted baby handed to a baby farmer. I foolishly introduced her to certain of our philanthropic friends. But even the most advanced among them could not understand her at all, and some of them were made indignant by her admiration for the then cruel workhouse system. However, a considerable number of people who thought themselves socialists showed her kindness. Walter Crane drew an allegorical drawing for the prospectus of a school she wished to found, and which was founded, in Fitzroy Street. She was a born teacher, and believed all human ills could be, and would be, cured by the spread of education. She was distressed to find I did not know the names of all the French departments, and suggested as a reward for all I was doing for her, in the way of advice, and in exchange for my bold fights with her landlord who objected to the presence of the cats who then shared her room, she should give me a course of lessons. This kind suggestion was refused by me.

I learnt with surprise the subjects she was prepared to teach the pupils in her school; the languages alone included, in addition to French and German, Russian and Spanish. She did in the end manage to get together some forty children, belonging to every nationality, and she had six colleagues who all worked without a salary. For a while they were filled with enthusiasm, and hung on her eloquent words—for eloquent she was. But she was the only real teacher among them. She was sufficiently simple to believe these colleagues would remain with her as long as she cared to carry on the school; but after a time they all drifted away.

Though almost all the parents of the children could have afforded to pay a fee, with only four exceptions they each took advantage of the fact that the founder "left it to them."

Louise Michel had been a school teacher, and I admired the way she dominated, and how well she managed, her large class of unruly children. At the time she was teaching in, and running, this school, she was working each night on an encyclopædia which she hoped would simplify the education of the young all over the world.

I have known a good many women who have been in prison; Louise Michel was the only woman on whom prison left no mark. She was for years in the French penal settlement of New Caledonia, living and being treated as if she belonged to the lowest type of criminal. But her kindness of heart and vivid intelligence stood her in good stead, and even the guardians, as the wardens were absurdly styled, became fond of her. The Governor formed such a high opinion of *La Vierge Rouge,* as they all called her, that when she was about to leave for France, he offered her a high salary to stay on as head of all the schools in the convict settlement.

She would never allow there was anything particularly unpleasant in a prisoner's lot, so long as he had plenty of paper and ink, and was allowed to read books that interested him. After she had been taken over an English prison, she told her escort, to his anger and consternation, that she now knew the British penal system to be the most inhuman in the world.

During the time I knew her well, she shared more than one of Paul Déroulède's views, and I remember seeing her burst into hearty laughter when I pointed out to her they had a good deal in common. She was a pacifist but, in that like Déroulède, she considered the French Government the worst government in Europe, and felt sure a time would come when that government would be swept away as chaff before the wind. She also maintained the Third Republic was far more tyrannical, and far more of an oligarchy, than were the European monarchies of that day. She strongly resented the fact that while in Paris she had not been allowed to hold a public meeting, and often declared there had been more freedom of speech under the Second Empire. She longed for, and was certain she would live to see, the abolition of capital; and she told me I should live to see universal revolution, and the world, as we then knew it, disappear. In fact, Louise Michel can truly be said to have been the first of the bolsheviks, using the term as it is loosely understood.

She was past middle age when I knew her, yet her mental energy was astounding. Even at the time she was running her school, and writing the children's encyclopædia, she was also busily engaged on a novel which was to be called *Humanité*.

Louise Michel violently objected to the French marriage system, and yet, oddly enough, she did not approve of divorce, and actually looked forward to a time when, as she pathetically put it, so sacred a tie will only be entered into after mature consideration, and will, as a matter of course, be eternal. So there will be then, she argued, no reason why a priest or a mayor should play any part in the affair, as each of the contracting parties will have too high a sense of honour to feel any necessity for a vain ceremony.

After she gave up the school—or when it gave her up—Louise

Michel lived in extreme poverty. It was a real trial to me to go and see her, because of the ever-increasing number of stray cats with which she was surrounded. Still, I did see her quite often, and a French girl, named Charlotte, who was only a little better off than herself, became devoted to her. Charlotte came and saw her every day; cooked her food; and made vain efforts to tidy her room.

The love of this singular woman's life had been her mother. This was the more moving as the woman she loved so dearly did not share her political views. She once told me that the only thing she had cared to take with her to New Caledonia was a portrait of her mother, and her great happiness in coming back to France was seeing her mother again. But soon she was arrested and put in prison, and while she was in prison Madame Michel died. This roused French public opinion, and Louise suddenly became so popular that the Musée Grévin had a waxwork showing *La Vierge Rouge* sitting in her cell, engaged in writing her mother's life.

She was exceedingly fond of music, which she read with ease, and I went to some trouble to obtain her certain scores. I used also to provide her with French books. Strange to say, though she could not speak English, she could write it really well, as the following—the only letter she ever wrote to me in English—will prove:

"Dear Miss,—I ask you to help the proscribed Spaniards, tortured and exiled though innocent, from their native land. Can you not draw up a letter to the papers asking England in the name of justice to help these poor people?

"The Spanish refugees are absolutely without means, in a strange land of which they do not even know the language. What they need above all is the sort of hospitality so generously given by England to all who lack shelter and bread.

"I shall pay you a visit to-morrow about four o'clock, to tell you more about these poor people, and I remain, dear Miss, with my respects to your Mamma, Yours truly, Louise Michel."

The only time I offended Louise Michel was when I laughed merrily on hearing her exclaim she felt sure the moment work was no longer compulsory, every man, woman, and child would feel a longing to work, and that all the distasteful chores of the world would be done so quickly that there would remain plenty of time for amusement. She took my laughter rather ill-humouredly; and when I pointed out there surely would always be incompetent people in the world, she at once replied that such worthless folk would be left to their laziness and incompetence. In the ideal world she thought to be just round the corner, every one would be free to do exactly as they liked, but she felt certain the lazy and incompetent would feel sad and ashamed when they saw the contempt felt for them.

I have known many socialists, even anarchists, in my time. They included Prince Kropotkin, whom I met now and again in the houses of English friends. But after Louise Michel, the woman holding advanced views for whom I felt the highest regard was Séverine, as she was always called. Her name does not appear in any French biographical dictionary I have ever consulted, yet I think it may truly be said that for some years this Frenchwoman ranked with the great French journalists of the last century. Indeed if Henri Rochfort be excepted, there was no Paris publicist who possessed to the same extent the fiery eloquence, mordant power, and quick wit, of the writer who chose to call herself by so unusual a pen-name. When I knew her she was editress-proprietress of the socialist daily paper, *Le Cri du Peuple,* but she had served a hard apprenticeship in ephemeral journalism.

For many years Séverine was secretary to Jules Vallès. She

must have been an enchantingly attractive young woman, and I think Vallès, in the intervals of his arduous work for the cause to which he gave his life, must surely have loved her. Be that as it may, she cherished his memory, and carried on his noble efforts to better the lot of the poorest class of worker. When I knew her she was middle-aged, but filled with what seemed a boundless vitality, and with a large circle of friends consisting of, as was natural, more men than women, who even if sharing only a few of her advanced opinions, loved and admired her.

There was nothing bohemian about Séverine. She came of sound military stock; two of her great uncles were killed at Sebastopol, and her father at the battle of Gravelotte. At a time when socialism was looked at very much askance, she had held a unique place in Paris journalism, and exercised a wide influence while writing for *Le Journal*. She there organized an attempt to direct into the right channels the ever-ready alms of the charitable. It was difficult, ungrateful, and tiring work, and could only have succeeded had she had the interest and active help of the Catholic laity. But it would never have occurred to her to ask for that. Still, for a while, she did an immense amount of good, organizing in every poor working quarter of Paris a kind of private inquiry bureau to which were attached men and women who investigated the cases of those who applied for help. If the report as to a case was favourable, a donation was provided out of the funds she had in hand. These donations ranged from twenty, to two hundred, francs. She early arranged to have nothing to do with the monetary side of the scheme, which was taken over and administered by a philanthropic banker. She told me she had received valuable help from the rich Paris Jews.

Séverine lived in Montmartre, and worked in what looked like the big living-room of a Breton farmhouse. There she saw her friends, and would cook for them a good simple dinner, for she prided herself on her housewifely qualities. As a writer the world

was her parish; anything and everything provided her with subjects, and she had what has always seemed to me a feminine passion for lost causes. When the Duc d'Orléans was imprisoned for
having dared to return to France in the hope of being allowed
to do his army service, Séverine vigorously took his part, and
some lively correspondence passed between her and *le premier
conscrit de France*. He must have found it pleasant to receive,
while in prison at Clairvaux, letters from one of the most brilliant writers of her day.

Some idea of her nature and disposition may be gleaned from a
list she drew up of forty "real immortals." The list began with
the Bible, and included Juvenal, Dickens, Dumas *père*, Baude-
laire, Michelet, and Stendhal. The only book by a woman on the
list was a novel by George Sand.

I am glad to have met, in the early 'nineties, the famous
fortune-teller whose professional name, Madame de Thèbes, was
said to have been chosen for her by Dumas *fils*. It was widely
believed he was her father. If that is true, she must have been
born when he was a very young man, for she looked more than
middle-aged when I made her acquaintance. Like Old Moore, she
published an almanac each year, and my cousin, René Millet, once
quite lost his temper with an old friend who assured him that
Madame de Thèbes' predictions invariably came true. She often
gave parties which were attended by many distinguished Frenchmen who regarded her with affection and respect.

She received her clients in a tiny room hung with the red material known as *Andrinople*, and against this blood-red background were hung casts of the hands of many famous people
who had consulted her. She undoubtedly had some kind of occult power, though she always denied it, for she regarded palm-
istry as a science, and described herself as a palmist. Yet she
foresaw the fire at the Charité Bazaar; the illness of Edward the

Seventh just before what was to have been his Coronation; the sudden death of President Faure; and what I think was the most impressive of all, the discovery of radium. In my view she even foresaw the present war, for in 1899 she declared England would face the most redoubtable war in her history during the coming century. As was natural, when war broke out in 1914 many of the men and women who believed in her occult gift considered this prophecy had come true. I, myself thought so.

I also became acquainted with a great number of French-women who had made, or were making, their mark in art and in the theatre. One of my cousins gave me an introduction to Sarah Bernhardt, and though I saw her at intervals during the rest of her life, I particularly remember my first visit, when I saw her in a large room which might have been the hall in an English country house. There were a number of men and women there, not one of whom I knew or had ever heard of, and they all treated her as though she were an Eastern queen who must be flattered and fawned on. At that time she had taken up sculpture; her mind was full of it; and it was as if the theatre, and everything that the theatre meant, had receded, and hardly counted in her daily life.

The only time I ever saw her alone was when she came to London some years later. We then had a really interesting talk, and she spoke with pride and love of her son. She told me that one of her very real troubles was being constantly asked for advice by the parents of girls who wished to go on to the stage. She declared she had never met any young woman, lacking some direct association with the theatre, who could conceive of what the successful career of an actress really means in the way of hard work, and of abnegation of every kind. She drew me a painful picture of her own youth, and of the bitter disappointments she had endured until her acting in Coppée's poetic little play *Le*

Passant, had brought her favourable notice both from the critics, and from the Paris public.

Though I agreed, and agree, with everything that has been written as to Sarah Bernhardt's extraordinary gifts, I far preferred Judic as an actress and as a woman. For one thing, Sarah was an international figure; Judic completely French; and she had many of the fine qualities of the old-fashioned Frenchwoman. At the time I met her, she was about forty, and the darling of the Parisian public, yet she seemed to me quite devoid of vanity. Unlike Sarah, she delighted in the world of the theatre, and was always eagerly ready to encourage and help any girl who wished to become an actress. I introduced to her a girl whose parents had been killed in an accident, and who had brothers and sisters dependent on her. Judic's kindness and thought for this young stranger were, as I look back, astonishing, on the part of an extremely busy woman. I knew nothing of her private life, but she seemed to me to lead a far more ordinary existence than most of the actresses with whom I came in contact. She lived to be old, and went on acting to the end, and I much admired her finished performance of the elderly woman, wife to a great painter, in *La Massière*, the best play written by Lemaître.

A completely different type of actress, and regarded as being in a real sense the head of her profession, was Madame Bartet, one of the *sociétaires* of the Comédie Française. Marcel Bartet put her far above any player then acting in Paris. He especially admired her conscientiousness; and I remember his telling me that when she knew she was shortly to act the part of a woman belonging to the Legitimist world, knowing it was a world apart from the Paris of that day, she obtained a job as cloakroom attendant in a house in the Faubourg Saint Germain, so as to see how great ladies put on and took off their evening cloaks, the way they addressed one another, and so on.

Dejazet was the only actress of the nineteenth century I would

have given much to know. She must have been one of the most
delightful Frenchwomen who ever lived; her *Lettres à Fanfan*,
addressed to an officer she loved, and published after her death,
rank, to me, among the few exquisite love-letters published in
our time, and they bear re-reading again and again. Every actress
who had the good fortune to see her play, always attempted afterwards to act in the way she had acted, for the highest praise for
which any actress could hope, was to be compared with Dejazet.
She died, alas! when I was seven years old.

XIX

IN the late autumn of 1895, I went to France for the first time for many years with no thought of work in my mind. I was going to be married in the following January, and I had known it would give my mother real happiness for us to be once more together at La Celle Saint Cloud.

We were not accompanied, as we always had been before, by Mrs. Mew, the old nurse who had played so great a part in my own and my brother's lives. This was a relief to me, for Nurse always looked grieved and shocked if everything about her, and in every room in whatever house we dwelt, was not as clean as a new pin. As it was, we had our meals brought in from the village inn, and I kept tidy the four rooms in which we lived.

I found it a poignant experience to slip back into my two very different pasts. The past of my childhood, and the nearer past, when I had been seventeen, and had returned, with a feeling of such intense joy, to the village which contained my happiest memories—indeed I might truly say what had been, till then, the only happy memories of my life.

Everything now appeared the same as it had done in the 'seventies, and in 1885; I, alone, had changed. But as it was after the *Jour des Morts* and the *Toussaint*, the houses of which the interiors had been so familiar during the last summer of my real youth were all empty and shuttered. I did not miss those who had been my contemporaries, and who had then taken me to their hearts. They seemed, indeed, to belong to another, and to an entirely different, existence, so completely had I myself altered in the eight years. Mine had become a working life and, with exceedingly few exceptions, the friends I had made in London were all, like me, workers, and almost all writers. With Jeanne Déroulède as the only exception, all the French girls I had known in 1885 were now wives and mothers. I did not know, in any real sense, a single married woman in England of my own age.

There was but one thing quite unchanged in my life. This was my relationship with my mother. She, herself, was the same as I had always known her. She appeared unaware of the material discomforts of the little house at Slindon to which she had now moved with Nurse. There was a tiny lawn which commanded a marvellous view of land, sea, and sky; and this view, seen from her bedroom and sitting-room, evidently made up to her, in a very real sense, for the bitter cold in winter, and the great heat in summer.

From when I was nineteen, I had made myself responsible for the house in Great College Street, Westminster. There my mother had been able to come at any time; and it had not occurred to her that my marriage would necessarily alter this arrangement, as it had certainly occurred to the circle composed of the feckless, idle, and selfish people whom she seemed to attract wherever she happened to be. Even if she had realized the fact, it would have caused her no distress; she had always been a visionary, a being who seemed to live in another dimension to that where dwelt ordinary men and women. But, in this unlike any other visionary I have known, she was always eager and ready to help those who believed they had been ill-treated by fate.

One thing had happened since she and I had last been together at La Celle Saint Cloud which made us both very happy. This was my brother having done well at Oxford. Indeed I think this fact shed a light which lasted till the end of her life. But as to my coming marriage, she felt none of the interest and excitement the normal mother then felt in such an event in a normal daughter's life. It gave her pleasure that my future husband was a member of *The Times* staff, because her father had been a friend of Delane, and had occasionally written a leader on some legal subject for the paper. But she never alluded to the kindness Mr. Lowndes (as she called him up to the day of my wedding) had shown, and the great trouble he had taken, when it had been made possible, some years before, for Hilaire to go to Oxford. She and I had known nothing of the procedure to be employed; the very few people to whom she had confided her intention not only disapproved (her trustee felt so strongly as to what he wrote to be the folly of the scheme, that he tried hard to throw spokes in the wheel), they all thought my brother, who had then just finished his *volontariat* in the French Army, ought at once to start earning his own living, preferably in a bank. When they found his mother's decision remained unshaken, it evidently never occurred to any one of them to help or advise her. Alone the man I had at the time refused to marry told her what to do. He drafted letters to certain heads of colleges, and went into the whole question as to the best course to pursue, in view of the fact that Hilaire had left the Oratory School four years before.

The influence this kindness had on my brother's life was inestimable, and the two men, so unlike in almost every way, became and remained, during the forty-seven years which followed, friends to the day of my husband's death.

But, at the time, the great kindness which had been shown by the man I was so soon going to marry, was as if blotted out. As, however, my mother would have done exactly the same had she been young Mr. Lowndes, instead of middle-aged Madame Belloc, all he had done did not strike her as being out of the way, and she did not mention him once during our stay at La Celle Saint Cloud.

Perhaps even more than was true of me, she may have felt as if she had slipped back into the past, for what had been the pattern of our daily life became at once the same as in my childhood. She made her own early cup of tea; then she spent the morning writing to friends in England; we had our simple lunch about eleven, and, after about an hour, we walked down to Bougival to catch an early post for our letters. We were home by three, and then came the making of what we thought of as our after- noon tea. After I had washed up the two cups and saucers, and emptied the silver gipsy-kettle teapot which had been one of my mother's cherished wedding presents, given to her by the dearly loved Quakeress, Mary Merryweather, after whom I had been named, we would sit down in the *grand salon*, and talk and read till dinner-time.

During this last stay at La Celle Saint Cloud, my mother talked to me, far more freely than she had ever done, of her life with my father, and, after his death, with Madame Swanton Belloc.

She once described, and it was the first time she had done so, what our house had looked like, and especially what the *grand salon* had looked like, when she had first seen it in the spring of 1867. How everything there, unconsciously fulfilling Ruskin's ideal, had been beautiful or useful. There were low First Empire bookcases in which stood, what specially pleased her, the many volumes of George Sand's *Histoire de ma vie*; and the comfortable furniture dated from before the Great Revolution. The parquet floor on which stood the chairs on which we had sat in 1895, was the only thing in the room which looked exactly as it had looked then, although it was of course a new parquet floor put there after the Prussian soldiers had made a fire in the centre of the room, thus risking burning down the house. The winter of 1870–71 had been exceptionally cold, and the fireplace, where only wood was burnt, must have seemed inadequate to men ac- customed to the stoves which even then were in every German living-room.

As long as I had known the *grand salon*, there was a plain

mirror above the chimney-piece. But my mother told me that before 1870–71, there had hung there, on the deep red wall, an enchanting picture of Aunt Lily as a child of six and, opposite the French windows, two fine portraits. The one was of my great-grandfather in his uniform as last Colonel of the Berwick Brigade (a picture evidently sent to Germany as loot, by some Prussian officer), the other that of his only son, Captain Armand Swanton. This picture, hidden by a kindly village friend early in the German occupation, is now in my brother's house in Sussex.

Always my mother came back, in talk and in thought, to the full-length portrait of my French grandmother which had dominated the *grand salon* during the first three years of her married life. It had been painted when Louise Swanton Belloc was thirty-two and, in the eyes of those who saw her then, even more beautiful than she had been during her girlhood. In this picture she is shown sitting by a writing-table, while against her knee leans her little daughter Lily, and at the child's feet is a gaily-coloured harlequin doll. To the right, in the shadow, behind the mother and child, is the dim shape of the painter before his easel. After her return to her ruined home in the late spring of 1871, my mother never once walked into the room without a pang of pain at missing this picture she had so loved. She refused to go and see it after it had been hung in the Louvre; and when she was given an engraving of the portrait, she quickly hid it.

So completely did my mother go back to the past, during those few days we spent together, that she would allude to certain pictures which I knew had either been destroyed or stolen by the Prussians as if they were still in the house, and she sometimes seemed distressed and surprised to find them missing from the walls of our living-rooms.

On a late afternoon she suddenly told me of something strange which had happened the autumn folowing my father's death.

She was sitting, one evening after dinner, in the *grand salon*, with Madame Swanton Belloc and Mademoiselle de Montgolfier. They had not lit the candles, or had a lamp brought in; dusk was falling, and the windows were still wide open. After a while my mother thought Mademoiselle must be feeling chilly, so she got up, and after shutting the high green shutters, she lit two candles. They were thinking of going to bed, when suddenly there came loud knocks which sounded exactly as if they had been made on one of the shutters by a tall man standing outside on the balcony.

Adelaide de Montgolfier did not move; she sat, a tiny, fragile figure, in a low chair, her face set and expressionless. But my mother and Madame Swanton Belloc got up at once and called out, "Who's there?" Receiving no answer, they flung open the shutters of both windows. It was almost dark by now, but light enough to see that there was no one on the balcony. They stood outside for a while, expecting to hear footsteps in the garden below. But no sounds broke on their listening ears, and at last they shut and barred the shutters. But as soon as they had sat down, they began hearing knocks coming from all parts of the room, and from the ceiling as well.

My brother and I were sleeping in the rooms above where the three women had been sitting, and my mother ran and opened the door of the little hall where was the corkscrew staircase which led up to our nurseries.

By now she felt sure the knocks had come from there. But she found us both sound asleep, and the knocks had ceased. Down she came, and at once the quick insistent sounds began again.

Then something took place which to two of those there seemed stranger, far, than what had just disturbed them. Mademoiselle de Montgolfier rose from her chair, and her face, which had so altered since my father's death as to seem that of another woman, became what it had once been, and as if illumined with

joy. But silence fell on the large room, and suddenly Mademoiselle's face became again as if drained of all thought and feeling,
while she slowly sank down into her low chair.

We found one change which affected my mother more than
myself. *Chez l'Empereur* had been bought from the Empress
Eugenie by the son of Monte Carlo Blanc. He kept his racehorses
there, and so naturally allowed no one access to the wild wooded
stretch of land where our parents had taken their last walk before they left La Celle Saint Cloud in the August of 1870.

One day was spent by us in Paris, and on that day Aunt Lily
asked all my cousins to lunch. Mamma was surprised at the intense interest they all showed in my coming marriage, and I saw
how astonished, on her side, was my aunt, at the little knowledge
my mother appeared to have acquired of my future husband, his
family, and friends. Though filled with a love which brought
with it such understanding, she was amazed that a woman she
knew felt as tender an affection as my mother felt for me, should
seem to take, as a matter of course, so great a change as marriage
must surely bring into my life. As for my other relations, while
genuinely attached to their Aunt Bessie, they put down everything odd or peculiar about her to the fact that she was an Englishwoman.

Apart from that one day in Paris, we stayed quietly at La
Celle Saint Cloud, seeing no one but our village friends, and
les bonnes sœurs, as the nuns were called. The older sisters had
all known my father, and one of the two, now an old woman,
who had spent the night praying by his body the night before
his burial, was still alive. Her gentle-looking unlined face,
framed in a white coif, remains with me as if she stood before
me now.

The postman was the same man I had known all my life,
though he was now old instead of young. *Monsieur le Facteur,*

as the maids had taught me to call him when I was a child, had always played a very important part in our household; and, as far as I was concerned, he did so more than ever now.

As had always happened every day, as long as I could remember anything, in the middle of the morning the bell by the side of our gate would tinkle, and I ran out eagerly, to hear exclaimed in a tone of great surprise: *"Encore une lettre pour vous, Mam'-selle Marie!"*

The old man must have noticed that on the flap of every envelope addressed to me was a mysterious little engraved double circle with *Printing House Square* within the rim; *1785* engraved in the centre; and *The Times* above and below *1785*. But though curiosity is a French trait, he was one of nature's gentlemen, and never inquired what all that signified.

After he had trudged on towards the village, I always put the precious letter into my pocket, and hastened back to where my mother was sitting writing in the *grand salon*. There I would leave her, and after walking through the dining-room where hung the old copy of Poussin's famous painting "I, too, have lived in Arcadia," stop before the door of the only other sitting-room in our house.

I had always been very fond of the square, peaceful-looking apartment we called the *petit salon*. There was a dark-green paper on the walls, and the small First Empire furniture was upholstered in green silk, and even the carpet, which would be looked on with horror, now, pretended to be moss.

After giving up Mrs. Parkes' house in London, my mother had taken to La Celle Saint Cloud two Italian paintings, and a portrait of Mirabeau, all three formerly in her father's collection of pictures, and she had had them hung in the *petit salon*. There was also there an oil sketch of a boat in which sat and stood a group of young people—the Hilaire Bellocs and some of their friends in the 'thirties. It was extremely artificial, while also ex-

tremely charming. The man who had painted it, Louis Boulanger
—in his day a well-known artist—had put himself, a palette in
his hand, among his sitters.

What was delightful to me in this sitting-room was the feeling of air and space with which it was filled. The one large window was shaded, on the left, by the wall of our tower; otherwise
it commanded the same view as did all the windows on that side
of the house. And there was a singular, to me an enchanting, feature, in the *petit salon*. It is a feature I have only seen in two other
rooms, each of them in an English country-house. This was a large
clear piece of glass set in the outside wall, above the black marble
mantelpiece. Through that piece of glass was a noble view,
bounded on one side by the aqueduct of Marly, and the long, far-
away terrace which forms the edge of the Forest of Saint Germain, while far below lay the wide valley of the winding Seine.

Incrusted in the wall on that side of the house was the round
bas-relief, sculptured by her elder daughter, of Madame Swanton
Belloc. If the Nazis who are now using the château of La Celle
Saint Cloud as a G.H.Q. have gone as far, they will have torn out
the bas-relief, for the name of Belloc is naturally anathema in
Germany.

But during those quiet days, in the peaceful France of my
young womanhood, I forgot, for the time being, both the past
war and the certainty of a coming war. And every morning, in
the *petit salon*, I would read an amusing, loving letter, always
filled with an eager longing for my return to what was still my
mother's house in Westminster, but where the writer and I were
to begin our married life, for of that little house my future husband had just acquired a sixty years' lease.

And yet while deeply moved, and aware of my singular good
fortune, I felt it strange and unnatural that the Englishman who
had cared for me with so patient and faithful an affection since
we had first met at Oxford when he was an undergraduate at